SECRET *freedom*

Praises for *Secret Freedom*

"Thank you for sharing your story at Res Life four months ago. It made me realize that I too needed to face the things in my life that still haunt me. Your transparency has given me courage".

–**STACY**, Conference Participant

"Ilonka's heartbreaking story is surpassed by her faith in a greater God. A redemptive read wrapped in amazing grace. A fresh breeze runs through the pages stirring hope. A story you won't soon forget."

–**PATSY CLAIRMONT**, International Speaker and Author of *You Are More Than You Know*

"I had the pleasure of hearing Ilonka speak and sing at two very different ladies events at my church this past year. One thing that stands out in my mind about Ilonka is how her heart and her message were cross generational and she was able to speak to women's hearts who were of different age groups and in very different places in their lives, and they all came away touched. I truly believe (and have seen evidenced) that women walked away changed because of the sweet, honest spirit and message that Ilonka was able to present both through her speaking and also through her singing. One friend whom I invited is going through a lot of difficult times in her life and wasn't sure she'd even enjoy being there at all. She walked away that night telling me that it was one of the most amazing evenings she had ever experienced. I fully recognize that this is not Ilonka alone, but the Holy Spirit working through her, but she had to be willing to be used. I appreciate her willingness to let the Lord use both the good stories and also the very difficult stories from her life to speak to women's hearts about the redeeming grace and love of God."

–**EVA**, Washington State

"Don't you find it interesting how God can take the broken pieces of our lives and not only weave them together to make something beautiful, but use those pieces to be an encouragement to others? The book you're holding is the story of a friend to whom that happened. Her life was in shambles and emotional torment, when she became personally acquainted with Jesus Christ, who not only redeemed her but also opened the door to healing, hope and happiness. As you encounter the transparency of this author, you'll see the value of being totally honest within yourself and how that honesty will continually build a great relationship between you and your Savior."

–**LUCI SWINDOLL**, Author/Speaker Women Of Faith

"If it hadn't been for Ilonka Deaton, I would have never thought there was help for me and other women like me…through this women's story and personal Skype video to me on the day I was forever changed! Redemption is possible.

–**HEATHER**, Human Trafficking Survivor

"Ilonka's story is one of my favorite stories in the whole history of Christ Community Church! I am so humbled that God allowed me to be part of the "unveiling hope" to her, and to see how Jesus, alone, shows us "what becomes of the broken hearted."

With much love and respect."

–**SCOTTY SMITH**, Founding Pastor of
Christ Community Church Franklin TN
and author of *Unveiled Hope*

SECRET
freedom

How *to* Fly Again
and Gain Freedom *from*
Keeping Secrets

Ilonka Deaton

NASHVILLE

NEW YORK • LONDON • MELBOURNE • VANCOUVER

SECRET *freedom*
How *to* Fly Again *and* Gain Freedom *from* Keeping Secrets

© 2019 Ilonka Deaton

Published in New York, New York, by Morgan James Publishing. Morgan James is a trademark of Morgan James, LLC. www.MorganJamesPublishing.com

The Morgan James Speakers Group can bring authors to your live event. For more information or to book an event visit The Morgan James Speakers Group at www.TheMorganJamesSpeakersGroup.com.

ISBN 978-1-64279-043-6 paperback
ISBN 978-1-64279-044-3 eBook
Library of Congress Control Number: 2018939246

Cover Design by:
Rachel Lopez
www.r2cdesign.com

Interior Design by:
Bonnie Bushman
The Whole Caboodle Graphic Design

In an effort to support local communities, raise awareness and funds, Morgan James Publishing donates a percentage of all book sales for the life of each book to Habitat for Humanity Peninsula and Greater Williamsburg.

Get involved today! Visit
www.MorganJamesBuilds.com

I dedicate this book with love to every individual who wants freedom from keeping secrets.

—Ilonka Deaton

Table of Contents

Foreword

Hush…I demanded.

Sit in your dark corner and don't say a word. Not a word. Haven't you harassed me enough? Your sulking and skulking all hours of the day and night troubling my mind with your hissing breath of accusations. Shame I'm fed up with you!

Have you ever felt that way? Emotionally crowded by voices of shame?

We've all battled with dark memories to some degree whether from long ago or last week. And some of us have paid the price of our own self-respect. Secrets have obscured our value, interfered with relationships, held us accountable for the actions of others, clouded our beliefs, and even made us sick.

Ilonka's story will unsettle you and encourage you. She will enlighten you and cheer you through your hidden passages toward the Light. She knows what it means to be a prisoner of someone's sin, to buy into a pack of lies, and to be bullied by her thoughts. And she knows the path to freedom.

I first met Ilonka when she took a side job of cleaning homes. Our home was one of those. She arrived at my front door and an instant kinship began. She would clean and we would visit. Soon she was attending a poetry class in my home, and as they say, the rest is history.

Ilonka is beautiful and full of mercy. Oh, and did I mention her voice? Not only does she have a lyrical South African accent, her singing voice is exquisite. So when she asked to take a poem I had written and set it to music I had no idea the words could sound so luminous and moving. But then Ilonka has paid a great price for her freedom which caused the strains of liberty to go deep within her and they seem to reverberate in everything she does. I've personally played "our" song for dozens of people and each one of them wept. It's that kind of experience.

I encourage you to lean into the honest words she shares about her darkest moments and the bright breakthrough to hope as she learns and invites us to Fly Again.

—**Patsy Clairmont**, Author of
You Are More Than You Know

Free Gift

I would like to give you a free gift of the song "Fly Again. Loved Still" that I co-wrote with my husband and Patsy Clairmont.

You can download this song by visiting
www.ilonkaministries.com.

Click on the tab at the top that says Fly Again and follow the instructions for your free song download.

I pray this song blesses you as you Fly Again in your life.

Introduction

What is your secret?

How long have you been keeping it?

There is no way to sugarcoat secrets. Wherever there are secrets, there is the sin. Wherever there is a sin, there is also the shame. Secrets are birthed in darkness and are expected to remain in the darkest part of our hearts, leaving very little room for the light of healing and grace to come in. If you are a secret keeper then you know you are in the battle for your very life. It threatens every aspect of your existence and it takes center stage of who you think you are. When that secret pops up in your mind, your tummy starts turning and you can feel the tingle in your chest that only reminds you to hide it again. This is a perpetual cycle that continues to bind many hearts into a self-reliant existence instead of a life filled with Grace and resting. Reading this paragraph probably makes you want to run, shut the book and walk away. I'm urging you to stay. Visit with me through these pages. You will find your own secret freedom that will bring resting and relief.

There are some big secrets such as abuse, trauma, abortion, infidelity, divorce, suicidal thoughts, aggression, and addiction. Then there's also some of the everyday secrets, financial struggles, depression, anxiety, marriage problems, dysfunction in family relationships, mental health, bitterness, un-forgiveness, resentment, anger and you name it. Pretty much anything that is stuck in your heart and has trapped you in silence; the very thing you don't talk about. Regardless if your secrets are big huge mountains or everyday life ones, they still remain a dark place that will bind you in shame, guilt and condemnation. Those are the very things Jesus came to give his life for, so that you wouldn't have to carry them. A shameful, guilt ridden and condemned life is not what God has in mind for us. Rather, He has resting, peace, love and freedom for us. The biggest lie of the enemy is to make you believe that you are the only one going through this, that no one would understand you and only judge you and that you are somehow unloved by God because of it. The Devil is a liar and thief who doesn't know the awesome plan God has for your life. He knows that as you experience and grasp the fact that God loved you first and as you are, that all shame, guilt, fear and condemnation will flee. None of the negatives can stand in the presence of God's grace because Jesus already paid the price in full for us.

Another misunderstanding of keeping secrets is that when you do decide to come clean with it, you have to tell the whole wide world about it and shout it from a rooftop so that it's not a secret anymore. This is incorrect. Keeping secrets is a spiritual thing first. It's between you and God. When sin and secrets take place in our lives the first offense is to God. No matter who created the offence, there is still an open wound that needs healing, so that is where you start with coming clean with any sin or secrets. When King David took Bathsheba to be his own and had her husband killed, he came clean with God and said this "Against you, you only, have I sinned and done what is evil in your sight" Psalm 51:4. This is where forgiveness, healing, freedom and redemption from secrets and sin take place, with God first. Regardless of whether the sin that caused your secrets was inflicted by you or someone else it has the same effect on your relationship with God. It causes hiding and shame. One of the first examples of this is in Genesis when Adam and Eve in the Garden of Eden hid from the Lord. They had sinned and knew it. They felt guilty and exposed. This is the same thing we do when we have secrets. We hide from God. We are filled with shame because sin happened and then we turn away from God. Sin, darkness and keeping secrets makes you turn away from God. We think we only hide it from the ones we are trying to protect but in fact, it is the turning away from God and holding the secret in the darkness that traps us.

For we cannot live a life free with Christ and hold secrets from Him. Now some will say what is the big deal because God knows everything anyway about our lives. As true as that is, God calls us into a relationship with Him and wants us to communicate with Him. This is not so that He would love you more, for He already loved your perfectly first. This is to help you live a life of hope and freedom and not devastation and harm. The Father wants you to trust Him enough to tell Him what's in your heart.

The Apostle Paul in 2 Corinthians 4:2 calls us to renounce secrets and shameful ways. Renouncing these secrets and shameful ways are not to aid you in obtaining mercy or grace from Christ. You have already been given that! You live not under a performance-based acceptance law but under grace itself. Renouncing secrets is to help aid you in the healing of your heart so that the light of Jesus can shine in all of those areas of your life.

Women are great secret keepers. It's really unfortunate that we are this good at it, for it shackles us to the lies of the enemy. It distorts our view and keeps us from God's best for our lives. I want God's best for my life and any secret keeper would tell you they also want to have the same thing; peace, freedom and a sound mind. There is a suffering that takes place in the silence of keeping a secret. This suffering begs for the story to be told of the origins of your secret. This suffering is also the one that wreaks havoc on your emotional and physical health. Suffering in this type of silence while keeping secrets would be the same as knowing you have a wound that needs critical care, yet doing nothing to treat it.

The urge and need to control a secret comes naturally. This control seems to be a safeguard, a gatekeeper, a nice fenced in area you get to hold on to. This type of control also confuses the lines between keeping a secret and holding confidentially. Those are vastly different. Secrets being the one that makes us turn from God, but confidentiality gives us the freedom to take that matter to God in prayer. One is inviting and the other is shaming.

You have heard the saying that is used in marriage "better the devil you know than the one you don't know." Applying that to your secret, I can see and understand how managing and controlling your secrets might seem to be better. But what if you don't have to settle for that. What if there is another option? One that gives you freedom. The good news is there is. It's found in your direct relationship with the Father and choosing confidentiality rather than keeping a secret. This is your secret freedom, your key to unlock and heal what has been a burden to you for so long.

I want you to learn how to fly again with a broken heart, with a new voice that will lift your wings again. I want you to experience the freedom I have felt with the Lord. *"The LORD is near to the broken hearted and saves the crushed in spirit." Psalms 34:18*

What has broken your heart and trapped you in a secret?

Swans are purely a symbol of true love. For each Swan there is only one partner. They mate for life or until that partner dies. It has often been found that when a Swan's mate has in fact died, it's not long after that the loss and grief overwhelms the partner to death of a broken heart itself. Not only are Swans a species that love their partner well and have strong relational bonds, but they also take care of their young with loving care and diligence. The bonding that happens between these two beautiful creatures speaks truth about our human experience of sharing love, affection and companionship in relationships.

Looking at beautiful birds such as these whose hearts can be broken, reminds me of when God saw that Adam was alone and that it wasn't good. Can you imagine what it must have felt like for Adam to name all the animals who all had their partners but there was none one for him? Thankfully, God being a gracious Father, blessed Adam with a mate. Someone he could love and cherish and experience life with. We all long for this. Through the fulfillment of Adam and Eve's love, their story itself is not without having broken hearts. Putting aside the fall of mankind, which is a biggy no doubt, look with me at the loss and grief both Adam and Eve went through. First, they were separated from God, which must have been such a lonely feeling. That was followed with them being the first parents to experience homicide in their family and they became the first parents to bury a son. Oh the debilitating grief and pain must have been awful.

Each of us owns a story of a broken heart. Whether it is by the loss of a loved one, a divorce or a friendship that took a wrong turn, we all know the sting of a breaking heart. Just like the Swan, we all long to have relationships that are pure, unbroken, everlasting bonds. After all, we have been created as relational beings.

My heart has been broken several times over several situations in my life. Two in particular stand out in my mind. One was when someone I trusted, sexually violated me and kept me in sexual slavery for five years. The other was when my eyes were opened to the reality that I had been the source of other's heartaches. My heart was overwhelmed and struck with the reality of pain in this fallen world. The reality of our fallen nature and the humility that comes with it exposes a deeper need that we all have… a need for a Savior.

You see, from the beginning of time God has been for us, and our enemy, Satan, has set out to destroy every beautiful creation God has ever made. The enemy wants to separate us from the very thing that we need, love, find comfort in and long to have relationship with, our Heavenly Father. Unfortunately the Devil is very sly and uses cheap attractive tactics to pull us in. For me it was the notion of having a father figure in my life when I desperately needed a Father. For you it is something else. However, as attractive as it seemed it is always a false lure, a slanted image created to draw us in only to break our hearts.

This is where God steps in. He is the healer of all broken hearts and trapped secrets. For no matter what the enemy has planned or executed against you God, already has a plan for comfort and redemption. I weep at the image of Jesus' heart breaking when Lazarus died. How much more does He then not weep for us when we experience a grief He never intended for us to have in the first place.

Walking with the hurt and pain of a broken heart can be debilitating and can also last for years if left unresolved. The process of healing from a broken heart can be a tough road, just like it is for the Swan who has lost a partner. The only way a Swan can survive after loosing a partner is to find another one. We all need healing when we break, and there is only one who can walk you into this healing place, our precious Jesus. Only when we collapse and fall on Him with all our tears and sadness and surrender our broken hearts to Him does the healing begin. I am not going to pretend that this is an easy process. It is not. The intimacy however that we get to experience, when holding onto to Jesus for dear life to heal us, brings forth a communion like you can not even imagine; sweet and pure to the comfort of our souls.

This is why I refuse to remain in this darkness as a secret keeper or a victim with a broken heart, but instead be victorious over my difficult story and seek freedom daily. For there is a way, a process for you too to gain the freedom you need to live the life God has intended for you to live.

A life without guilt, shame, fear, condemnation, darkness, depression, anxiety, suicidal thoughts, not feeling enough, not knowing your true worth and feeling all alone. This is exactly how the enemy wants you to feel and operate; from a place less-than, but God has bigger and better plans for you. He likes to use our stories to be glorified through us. Therefore you operate from a place of strength and more than enough.

Facing the tragedies of your past will help you to start unfolding your story. As you do this, you will be able to pick up the pieces, beautiful and hard, and claim them as your own. Facing your past and what has brought you to this place of holding secrets will help you in the process of naming what your needs are. If your need, for instance, is to forgive or receive forgiveness, you will then be able to take that specific need to God for help. However, you can't name your need if you have not faced the reasons of why those dark lonely places exist in your heart. The more you become a student of your story, the greater your freedom will be. For only then can you learn to listen to your heart and step into freedom with a posture of surrender and humility.

Listening to your heart is key to your healing process. As you do this, you will step into the four crucial places with God; repentance, surrendering, renouncing and forgiveness. In Mathew 11:28 Jesus invites us to collapse onto Him when we are weary and burdened and He will give us rest. When we turn towards God and surrender, He meets us with comfort, never a sharp tongue or with a whip in his hand. Rather, a loving understanding that we are like sheep and need help. In renouncing the secrets of your past, God will bring forth a new forgiveness and life from you. We are broken, then blessed, and then used to help others. It might seem that this is a 1-2-3 process but it's more of a choreographed dance that the Holy Spirit leads and it just happens as your heart is willing. God is so faithful to meet you right where you are, exactly just as you are today.

After you have entered this process which I like to call, "coming clean with God", you will get to the "now what?" phase. With healing comes new life, new revelation, new callings and new beginnings. 2 Corinthians 1:4 says "*God comforts us through all of our troubles so that we can, therefore, go forth and comfort others with the same comfort God has given to us*". That means that God is equipping you through your own secrets and story to go forth and help others. This is a beautiful thing because as you do this, God will be glorified through you. It is powerful. This is how we overcome evil, by the Blood of the Lamb and the word of our testimony. As you enter into this phase it will be important for you to write your story, unwrap your shame, and obtain a posture of being guiltless; understand true grace, seeing your true identity, reclaiming your worth, your identity and then going forth and using your story as God leads you.

Through your commitment and courageous steps to turn once again to God with these most difficult places in your heart, you too can experience awesome freedom. I want you to fly again in your life. I want you to use your voice. I want for you to see how deeply you matter to God and that He has never and will never leave you. You are not alone in your process as you start to look at what's in your heart. He is with you every second and every step of the way. Just as I have, you can do this! No secret is worth more than keeping your redemptive relationship and freedom with Christ. I look forward to journeying in your process with you as we move forward. You can do this!

Phase I

Your Secret

Chapter 1

Being A Secret Keeper

Looking at the secrets trapped in your heart

"Lies and secrets, are like a cancer in the soul. They eat away what is good and leave only destruction behind."
–Cassandra Clare

I wouldn't be so presumptuous to ask you to share your secrets with me if I wasn't willing to share mine first.

I had secrets, a secret that I kept for 12 very long years.

A secret so severe that it almost destroyed me as it requested my very life. A secret that would define the first parts of my adult life and one that shackled me to darkness. A secret that I vowed to keep in silence thinking I was protecting those around me and myself. A secret that overtook my identity

3

and became the only narrow focused life I lived, in order to survive everyday life.

My secret, unfortunately, is one that many others share with me. It might not be the exact same story line, but close enough in proximity to also hold this secret's narrative.

I grew up in a single parent broken family with my mom and two brothers in Johannesburg South Africa. My dad wasn't there. My parents divorced when I was 13 months old and my dad became absent. During the early years of my childhood the fear of the abandonment I felt left me wanting to simply *matter* in this world. I suffered from separation anxiety and felt lost. The sense to be wanted and loved was so strong that it became the lens I saw life through. I wanted to find a place where I too could fit. I did not know that the example I needed from my dad to establish my worth and value was not only absent but would cast a mirror image for me of how I was to view God the Father in my future. My earthly dad was a drunk and one that abandoned us, so naturally God took the same place in my mind. Mom, on the other hand, was there, worked her fingers to the bone to provide for us and loved us.

One of the ways I could express how I felt was through singing. I didn't have to justify it, I could just sing my heart out and feel better. I won a national singing competition when I was 12 years old. It was kind of like an American Idol but much smaller as South Africa isn't as large as the US. Actually, the whole country of South Africa can literally fit inside the state of Texas. This event changed the course of not only my singing career but also my personal life. For the first several months after winning the competition my life was great. I felt like I belonged. I felt that I mattered. My music manager who was an older man stepped into a place of being a father figure to me. I was living my singing dream and for the first time thinking I knew what it might have been like to have a dad.

This dream-like glitzy glamour cloud I was floating on came to a screeching halt when my music manager, that same man I started to trust, raped me. After this horrific experience, he threatened to kill my family and me if I said a word. I believed him. I vowed my silence. I had hoped that somehow I would never see him again and that this would never happen again, but I was wrong. He struck again and again. For the next five years of my life, I became trapped as his sex slave and also to whomever he wanted to sell me to for sex. The more I complied, the more money I made. In his manipulation, he always found a way to tie it into my music career, as if this is what you allow if you want to be a star. Sadly this happens to a lot of female artists who are in the rising years of their careers. His power and arrogance taunted the very fabric of my life. I couldn't stand him, but I also couldn't say a word. The longer time went on the worse my unhealthy co-dependency became. To survive what I was going through, I gave in and went along. My ambivalence between right and wrong grew with deeper strength up until the point that I lost myself and died emotionally. Once to that point, I went on autopilot.

During the five years of captivity to him, my mom knew that something was horribly wrong. She took me from counselor to psychiatrist, pastor to women's leaders in the church. Anything to reach me but I just would not speak. I still believed he would kill me, as his threat of that never let up. I can hear it now… "This will be our little secret." And so it was. I had become a master secret-keeper. I coped with finding friends who I felt were as screwed up as I was. I drank, smoked like a chimney and used occasional pot. My thinking became skewed as I viewed my body as something you use to get things. The closer I could be to people who would not judge me, the better I thought I would be.

When I was 17 years old, an undercover cop, who was moonlighting at a casino club I was singing at, rescued me. I recall this event from one of my journals, as it all too well explains who, what and how I had become.

Fighting For My Life

Murder. I never thought I would be capable of such a horrible act, but if he pushed me one more time, I might have done just that.

Taking one more drag from my slim menthol cigarette, I felt lifeless, distant, deprived of any power of sensation, and standing once again it a damn Casino in Johannesburg, a big swanky, grand, five-star resort in South Africa. Sitting on hundreds of acres, this glitzy place is one for the elite. It is surrounded by a pristine lush green golf course, as valets tend to limousines, Lamborghinis, Porches and Bentleys while the young, the beautiful, and the rich step out in furs and jewels to come and collect their fortunes. High rollers, living the charmed life, wearing gold chains and puffing on Cohiba Cuban cigars lined the tables. While flirting with the half-naked showgirls, they sipped their fine brandy. Eager managers prowled the floor promising lavish comps and perks in return for the dollars to keep on flowing.

Amazed at what my 17-year-old self-had become in this erotic place, I felt no excitement. Catching a glimpse of myself in the mirror, standing in the all too familiar dressing room I have been in countless times before, I loathed what I saw. I stuffed the red lipstick stained cigarette butt with my trembling hand into my half drank Coke can, cutting my finger. As I blew the remaining smoke across my lips, he came through the dressing room door.

Swaggering in, waving his hand through the air as if to get rid of it, he stammers,

"I h-h-hate s-smoke."

I didn't really care what he liked or didn't like. For all, I cared he could go to hell. Illuminating bulbs of light exposed every line of my frown. While attempting to apply some extra glossy lip-gloss, he places his hand on my shoulders. Here we go again. With no escape, between the glaring lights and his filthy expecting hands, I burned with anger like an atomic bomb getting ready to explode. Jilting my shoulders forward in rejection,

"I'm not doing this."

Staring at me with his piercing blue eyes, wearing a stupid ball cap, he grins, pulling a smile to the one side of his face exposing his protruding eyetooth. It compliments the arrogance of the chain around his neck and the ring in his ear. The sweet smell of his cologne combined with his sunflower, oil-like body odor made me sick to my stomach. He stood there in all his glory with his faded black jeans, black t-shirt and western belt buckle that he wore way too often. Protruding his head forward, looking like a 5'10" tortoise, he wasn't going to let up. Gaining confidence as he usually did, removing his stutter, he gripped me a little tighter.

"Come on, you don't have to go on stage yet."

"No! Leave me alone. I'm not doing this."

"You know there's a sweet lady here tonight who drove a long way to come and see me, but I would rather have you," as if his pathetic attempt to make me jealous by manipulating me would somehow persuade me that what he wants is ok.

Not this time. I'm done with this and wonder if these skanky, slutty women know he is a sick, disgusting freak.

"No!"

"You will do this, you will."

Grabbing my hair he yanks my head backward spinning me around to face him.

"Be a good girl."

I could feel the anger in his breath sliding across my face. Taking his thumb and rubbing it across my lips he smears red across my cheek. This is all a sick game to him.

"No, no, no… get off me."

Still having a hold of my hair he pulled my head, grabbed the strap of my evening dress, which was lined with rhinestones, and ripped it off. Jewels scattered everywhere, dropping the dress to one side. Pushing as hard as I could, I just could not break free.

"You are hurting me. Leave me alone."

I felt helpless, sad, angry and mad as a hornet. I didn't have any more tears, I just wanted to get away and be normal. Is that so much to ask for? I just want to have a normal life.

Violently tangled in a fight, which I knew would be for my very life, he managed to wrestle me to the ground, shouting obscene profanities.

Like a broken record my thoughts kept repeating.

"I will not let him rape me, I will not, I will not."

I didn't care if this was the last day I lived. I wasn't going to let him do this. Something inside me knew I needed to fight back and not give in.

Suddenly there was a knock at the dressing room door.

"Ilonka, they are ready for you."

"Ilonka, is everything alright?"

The undercover cop who was providing security for me that night slowly pushed the door open.

"What the … stop, stop!"

It turned into three-person fight. The sight of it was like the worst of the worst on the Jerry Springer Show. Tensions grew quickly, anger escalated beyond what I could have ever imagined, and my sadness dropped a bowling ball into my gut.

How can this be my life? Am I not worth anything but only this? Will I ever be free from this torture? How did I get here?

It's been a long dark road that started years ago.

Keeping Secrets, **Ilonka Deaton**

After being rescued that day, I ran away from home and moved in with a stranger. It took my mom months to find me with the help of authorities. I just didn't know how to explain what had happened without coming clean with my secret. Once I got home, my mom then knew that strong intervention was needed from God to help turn this tide. She felt it in her heart to get me away from that environment and immigrated us to Nashville Tennessee after my graduating year of high school.

Arriving in Nashville, I walked into my young adult life with no idea who I was. I was filled with shame, guilt and depression that was pulling me down into a dark hole. Yet still, I kept my secret. If you have ever seen *The Lord Of The Rings*, when Gollum was holding the ring and saying, "My Precious", that is how I treated my secrets. Protecting the very thing for dear life that was busy killing me. Makes no sense, right? But here we are, and we all keep secrets. Just like Gollum holding onto his "Precious".

I ended up marrying the first guy who was nice to me and who didn't want anything from me. It was a bad idea and I should never have married him. Five years into that marriage my heart was consumed with darkness and I just couldn't keep the lid on my secret anymore. What triggered my secret was a conversation I overheard at the record company's office in Nashville that I was signed to. The president of the company, who today is my husband Bill, was having a conversation with one of his employees about the sickness of child abuse. They were talking about U. S. Senator Barney Frank and his endorsement of NAMBLA (The North American Man/Boy Love Association), a pedophilia advocacy organization in the United States. NAMBLA's goal, or one of them, is to abolish age of consent laws criminalizing adult sexual involvement with minors. Overhearing their discussion was the trigger that flipped a light switch inside of me and there was no pushing any of it back down again.

The months that followed were a bloody mess. I ended up having an affair with Bill, devastating my previous marriage, going through a divorce and ultimately attempted suicide. I ended up in a psychiatric hospital in Nashville for an extended period of time. Life was hell. Yet still, I was holding on to my secret. Though at this point people like Bill, my family and therapist started to know a piece of the narrative; that I wasn't ready to move from victim to victor yet. It took another six months for me to come to the end of myself.

In the spring of 2008, I finally turned to the only One who could heal my secret after hearing a pastor, Scotty Smith, preaching about the Grace of Jesus. That very day I cried out with all my heart and gave up my secret. It was the moment that I turned to God and surrendered the darkness of my secret to Him. That very day was the starting point of my healing. Before this day I tried everything you can imagine, medicines, treatments, physiatrists, psychologists and self-help books. None of those worked until the spiritual peace of surrendering to God came in. Only then did I start to heal. Sometimes in anger, we turn away from God because we didn't feel Him near when our secrets took place. Yet He is the very ingredient we need to succeed.

My 12-year-long secret almost destroyed me. But God had bigger plans for my broken story. For the last 10 years, I have been on a healing recovery journey that has changed my life and has brought me hope.

Yes, indeed today I am free. I feel like a songbird out of a cage and so can you.

It is my hope that as I share and walk through the process of what undoing secrets look like, and the process thereof, that you too will find the freedom and healing you need to live a life full of joy, redemption and filled with hope.

Let's get to work! This brings me back to important questions for you.

What is your secret?

How long have you been keeping it?

The answers might not be something you are ready to write down yet, but I do want you to answer these two questions in your mind.

As you think of them, let me pray for you:

Father God, thank you for this beautiful child you have created. Lord, I ask for your courage and boldness to help unfold the secrets and stories that need to be told here. Lord I also ask for you to help in our unbelief so that we can take the difficult steps. Thank you for your guidance and help as we share. Lord, cover your child with comfort and peace as we journey forward. In Jesus name, I pray for you, Amen.

Discussion Notes

At this point I would like for you to get a designated journal for this process, a journal that you can keep private and confidential. Journaling your answers and thoughts is very effective in processing what is in your heart and mind. Your secrets and thoughts are like a hamster stuck on an exercise wheel that is going round and round and can't stop. We need to give your secret and your thoughts a way to get off that exercise wheel. We need to give them a voice. When you write something down that is bothering you for instance, you are allowing your mind to say what it needs to say, and then you can rest. If you struggle with sleeping because your mind won't shut down or, if like me, have had arguments with people in your mind that goes on and on, journaling is so helpful. It gives you the ability to say what you need to say without any judgment or criticism. Ever felt like you just want to be heard? Journaling can provide this safe place for you to share.

Most of us make a shopping list when we go to the grocery store. Why do we do this? It is so that we won't forget of course. Have you ever noticed that once you have made your list you don't worry anymore about remembering what you need to buy? That's because it's on your list. You will take it with you and be reminded. Well, processing our emotions and secrets works the same way. As I have walked through my own healing I can honestly tell you that the most effective periods of healing and "ah-ha" moments I have had was while I was physically writing my story line by line.

Don't feel like you need to be in a rush. Take your time with this crucial step as you name your secrets and remember for how long you have been keeping them. Then move forward to the next chapter when you are ready. I am proud of you for journeying with me thus far. You can do this!

Chapter 2

Suffering in Secret

Finding the origins of your secrets

"Grace takes us through suffering. Remember, we are: Afflicted but not crushed. Perplexed but not despairing. Persecuted but nor forsaken. Struck down but not destroyed."

–Anonymous

Silence comes with a price. It causes a suffering that is isolating. It removes your ability to allow a healthy relationship to grow and prevents new ones from starting. It also keeps you trapped in a place that can pull you into a depression, like a bird in a cage with the door shut. This is *not* how God intended for us to live. When we are faced inwardly, focusing on all our own problems, we live in a very small world that presses down on us. When we lift up our eyes as Psalms 121:1-2 reminds us, *"I lift up my eyes to the hills, where does my help come from? My help comes from the Lord, the Maker of heaven and earth."* then we gain a bigger perspective that broadens our small worldview into a larger freedom of possibilities. This happens because the Lord himself, who absolutely adores you, has so much more for you than the inner turmoil that has been trapping you.

Suffering in secret is not a fun place to live. We have either met, or we have been the friend of, a child or spouse that keeps you at arms length. It's that uncomfortable knowing that there is a 10-foot wall to keep everyone out. We might think it's to protect ourselves but in actuality it is this very thing that the enemy uses to isolate you away from the life God has intended for you.

Amanda has been a friend of Tiffany's for the past two years. Their relationship has the potential to grow into a long lasting friendship. They both share a common interest, their children. They are the same age and get along just swell. Most times when Amanda comes over to Tiffany's for a play date, she does it with an ambivalent heart. She likes Tiffany on the one hand, but on the other hand, she gets jealous of the beautiful intimacy Tiffany has with her little girl. This display of affection and emotions makes Amanda uncomfortable because it reminds her that she had a mother who wasn't emotionally available to her. Tiffany can sense the walls Amanda puts up, but does not understand why.

One afternoon Tiffany had a moment of bravery and opened up to Amanda.

"Amanda, I have been experiencing this uncomfortable atmosphere when you come over for play dates. Is it my imagination or is something wrong?"

At first, Amanda did not know what to say. Being transparent with her feelings is not something she is used to doing. Her mother never gave her the example of how to be vulnerable. She thus follows the pattern of being emotionally unavailable.

"I am so sorry Tiffany. You see, I have this deep longing to have the kind of relationship with my mother that you have with your little girl. I guess it makes me jealous. My heart aches. I don't want to be jealous because it's beautiful. I don't know. My heart is just sad that I missed out on that and don't know how to fix it. It seems easier for me to just withdraw to myself when I feel this way."

"Thank you for sharing that with me Amanda. I am so sorry you didn't have that with your mom. Neither did I. My parents went through a divorce when I was a teenager and I blamed my mom for it. I was angry with her for many years. We had an estranged relationship. It was only after I got married that I started down a road of reconciliation with my mom. I made a promise to myself that if I ever had my own little girl, I would work really hard to be affectionate and intentional to have a healthy intimacy with my daughter. I never want her to feel the way I did."

This conversation transformed the relationship between Amanda and Tiffany. One moment of speaking the truth about a heart's secret allowed these two women to not only comfort each other, but to also start walking with each other in this struggle. Amanda gleaned from Tiffany's experience and started implementing some of the same choices of being intentional and intimate with her family. The change was so positive and obvious that Amanda's husband recognized it. Not only that, but Amanda also learned how to start approaching her mother with honesty about her feelings.

Amanda's secret is one that many of us hold. It's an everyday secret that shows up when we interact in friendships and relationship. Unfortunately, the brokenness from our families does play a role in our adult lives. Sooner or later that brokenness creates everyday secrets that need to be unveiled, addressed and processed. Amanda's story is just an example of how a parent-child relationship can shape a secret. The key for Amanda was to find the origins of why she felt the way she did. Once she could name it, she could speak it; bringing it from darkness into light.

Finding the origins of your secrets is so important. It will help you to, first of all, recognize the hurt, and then express the pain. More often than not, we can name the hurts of our past, but finding the roots of them can be most difficult to expose. Once you have found them, you can then address your need. If you are unable to see the root origins of what's causing your suffering, it's ok. This is a process. It is a learning curve of becoming a bit like an investigator of your own story; it takes time and being intentional with it. Be patient with yourself as you move through this and give yourself grace.

If finding the origins of your secrets is hard or unknown, then I recommend you pray this prayer and ask God for help. He is so amazingly faithful to help you. The Holy Spirit, who is called your Counselor, will bring you clarity.

> *Dear Heavenly Father,*
>
> *Thank you for your faithfulness. Thank you that I can come to you in my time of need. Father, please help me through your Holy Spirit to reveal to me the secrets that are in my heart and the origins of them. Please help me gently as I move through this and please remind me of Your new grace and mercies daily.*
>
> *In Jesus name, Amen.*

This is a powerful prayer, so be ready and on the lookout for what God is going to reveal to you.

I recently spoke at a conference teaching women how to start writing and sharing their stories. After one of the afternoon sessions, a woman came up to me and was pretty aggravated with a message I had taught on forgiveness. I had expressed in my message that if you have been hurt in your life and you still carry un-forgiveness, bitterness or anger in your heart toward the person that harmed you, you should consider turning and surrendering these difficult places to the Lord so that you can find forgiveness and freedom. She was very offended and angry. For confidentiality purposes we will call the woman Janine.

"Ms. Deaton, how can you even ask or recommend such a thing? My dad brutally sexually and physically assaulted me for most of my childhood. When I turned 18 and could leave I made a vow to myself that I would never forgive him for what he did to me. Never! How can you ask me to forgive such a monster?"

"Janine, I am so very sorry that happened to you. I can understand your anger. If I may ask, how is your relationship currently with your dad?"

"He died 25 years ago."

When she said that it gave me great pause and understanding for the hurt she has been living with. This was a hurt so deep that it was crushing her emotionally. Can you imagine the hell that she lives everyday being a prisoner to her dad's offences and sin against her?

"Are you married Janine or do you have a family of your own?"

"No, I don' trust men."

"I can understand that. Why would you think anything else when the only example you got of what men are suppose to be like was a beater and an abuser. This has also shaped your view of God."

"Well, I don't care. I have every right to hate my dad and to be angry."

Although Janine has the right to be hurt, feel betrayed and be angry, there is only one problem with this. She has been living with this darkness and anger for most of her life and it has robbed her of beautiful things. She is a prisoner to her own heart.

"Your request is preposterous and I will never ever forgive my dad."

In a heated moment of her anger, I took a bold step and pressed in deeper with her.

"I urge you to see that your un-forgiveness is holding you hostage and that the Lord wants to help you with this. Consider giving your pain, hate, anger, disappointment and un-forgiveness to The Father. I can to pray with you if you would like that.

"I will never forgive him!"

She stormed off furious with me. It was quite the scene.

My heart ached for her because I understood the effects of child sexual abuse and also what it is like to have a dysfunctional dad; the sexual abuse from my music manager, and the abandonment from my dad.

After my mom and dad got divorced when I was about 13 months old, he continued on in the Air Force in South Africa. He ended up having PTSD and became a dysfunctional alcoholic who wouldn't be around for months at a time and then show up drunk at my school events. I was sad, embarrassed and angry with him. I carried that anger all the way into my deep twenties when I was forced to give it to God and ask for help. I would not ask you or anyone that hears me speak, or who reads my words, to do something I haven't done. I can only relate and walk alongside of you from my own story and experiences. After I asked the Lord to help me forgive, He started giving me windows and opportunities to talk with my dad about how hurt and angry I had been. Forgiving my dad and having reconciliation was about a yearlong process from the day I asked the Lord to help me. It absolutely was worth it.

The next morning at the conference I was getting ready to teach again. That same woman, Janine, came rushing up to me with a smile on her face and crocodile tears running down her face. She hugged me without saying a word at first and I just knew what happened. She did it. She took a step of great courage and gave her darkest place, her secrets of un-forgiveness and bitterness to God.

"You won't believe it, God showed up for me last night. I feel free. After I had spoken with you last night, I went back to my room where I met up with my roommates. In my anger and being upset, three of the women surrounded me and offered to help comfort me. Their comfort turned into a couple of hours of discussion that led to me accepting their prayers and being willing to ask God for help. When they started praying, God gave me an extra portion of faith and I asked Him to help me forgive my dad. In that instance, God opened my heart and gave me the forgiveness I never thought I could have. I have never experienced God like this. It was as if He was in the room with us. When I think about my dad I'm not angry. I am just…I guess what I'm trying to say is I feel free. Like I might be able to move on."

She was set free from a dark secret vow she had made more than 40 years ago. Hallelujah and thank you, Jesus! What a remarkable story of God's healing power in our lives. You never know which sermon, CD series, bible study or conversation God is going to use to completely undo you and get your attention.

Whenever I get irritated or aggravated by something someone says, I try to pay attention to my own heart. I do this because most often I have something in my heart that needs to be dealt with. God uses the community all around us to help shape and mold us into what He has planned for us. He likes to use other people in our life to show us the condition of our own heart, and what needs to be worked on. So if you get triggered, aggravated or angry by something someone has said that hits home for you, pay attention because God is at work in you.

It's not all up to us. Yes we can make a decision to look into our brokenness, but we are unable to give forgiveness to ourselves or to those who have harmed us. We need God to *impart* that forgiveness to us so that we *can* forgive. But if we hold onto it and try to control the origins of the secret itself, we won't find the forgiveness from God, because we won't ask Him to take control of it. There is not one good thing that can come from suffering in secret. Taking that step of courage and surrendering your deepest past hurts to God brings healing.

If you are carrying anger, bitterness, and un-forgiveness in your heart, then the time has come for you too to consider surrendering those pieces to God and to ask for His help. No secret can maintain its power in the presence of God's Grace, because there is no condemnation for those of you who are in Jesus Christ. (Romans 8:1) When I notice that I have un-forgiveness, I pray this prayer:

Search me, O God and know my heart; if there is any hurtful way in me please lead me in Your everlasting way. Help my unbelief and help me to forgive. I surrender this un-forgiveness, this bitter hurt that I have to you, Lord. Now please rid me from this and make my heart like Yours.

Thank you, Father.

In Jesus name I pray.

You can use this prayer or create your own. God delights in helping us. So ask away and take the step of courage!

Discussion Notes

In the previous chapter, I asked you to start making mental notes on your own secrets and to get your first Discussion

Notes on paper. The first two questions were: What is your secret and how long have you been keeping it? The next two questions I want for us to address is:

How are you suffering in secret?

What are the origins of your secret?

Answer what you can. Take your time and use this as an opportunity to draw closer to the Lord as you unpack what is in your heart. If you can't answer them all, it's ok. Through the journey of this guide and process, you will be able to answer those questions in your own time as your heart is ready, and as God reveals your own heart to you. Remember to give yourself grace and time. Take your time and then let's move forward.

I am proud of you for journeying with me thus far. You can do this!

Chapter 3

Controlling Your Secrets

Looking at the effects your secrets have had on your life

"The more we let God take us over, the more truly we become ourselves."

–C.S. Lewis

How have your secrets affected your life?

Secrets can have a multitude of effects on our lives. It can manifest itself in different ways. For some people the effect could be emotional distress or physical ailments. Personally, I experienced emotional distress first and then later came some physical problems. If your secret has any kind of trauma connected to it, your experience will be vastly different than someone whose secret does not have trauma. Trauma has memory. There are extensive studies that have been done on how the body responds to emotional trauma. Dr. Dan Allender of the Allender Center at The Seattle School and author of *The Wounded Heart* describes it this way.

"Narration, story, is how we remember. You don't remember by what occurred, you remember by the way you narrate that experience. The phenomena of shame and ambivalence, and then a turn to contempt, judgment, and then a flight to dissociation, that's the normal standard, versus a heart able to walk into the particularity of the story where the shame is held, to be able to grieve when your body felt what it felt, and to do so now, in the present, with a kindness on behalf of that younger part of you. That is the work of redemption."

Ever feeling you have is somehow connected to a place in your body.

Let's look at Adam and Eve for a moment in the Garden of Eden when the serpent deceived Eve to eat from the Tree of Good and Evil.

Genesis 3:6-11 *"When the woman saw that the fruit of the tree was good for food and pleasing to the eye, and also desirable for gaining wisdom, she took some and ate it. She also gave some to her husband, who was with her, and he ate it.*

Then the eyes of both of them were opened, and they realized they were naked; so they sewed fig leaves together and made coverings for themselves.

Then the man and his wife heard the sound of the Lord God as He was walking in the garden in the cool of the day, and they hid from the Lord God among the trees of the garden. But the Lord God called to the man, "Where are you?"

He answered, "I heard you in the garden, and I was afraid because I was naked; so I hid."

And He said, "Who told you that you were naked? Have you eaten from the tree that I commanded you not to eat from?"

Here we clearly see the emotional effect of shame entering immediately into the minds of Adam and Eve when they ate of the tree *"and they realized they were naked; so they sewed fig leaves together and made coverings for themselves."* Before this moment they knew no shame, no nakedness. From this point forth the effect of the fall has been permeating peoples' lives and we all try to push back those effects to aid and help our hurting hearts. If you were to ask any ex-secret keeper which emotions they felt, more than likely the word *shame* is going to come up in the conversation. Shame is a natural occurrence that happens in the brain when secrets are present. Whether the person themselves did something wrong or wrong was done to them. The secret itself has the connotations to carry the emotional effect of shame into your life. Often with shame we find that people also feel tremendous guilt. Feeling that somehow, whatever happened, it's their fault, even when it wasn't.

I can clearly remember what it felt like to carry shame and guilt in my own life. Oh how thankful I am that that has been thrown off of me, for the weight of it is crushing. Take my secret, for instance, as I recount from my book *Keeping Secrets* on how I experienced guilt and shame.

Guilt

Guilt and shame are two of the hardest soul wounds I faced.

Feeling guilty is part of the soul damage that is ushered into your life with sexual abuse, or any abuse for that matter. Somehow we all think we could have done something to stop it, and find ways to blame ourselves. I use to think if only I wasn't so needy as a child who wanted a father, he probably wouldn't have raped me. If only I wasn't this way or that way is a dead end road that continues to loop in your mind for days on end with no resolve. Speaking my guilt and honestly getting to the roots of my feelings helped me understand. There is and will never be anything I could have done to stop what he did. The guilt of the sin doesn't lie with me but with him. Now saying this is easy but learning is an entirely different story. It took multiple conversations is counseling to get to this point. It's the undoing of wrongful thinking that lets us see the truth of correct thinking. To wish the situation away is natural but it's not practical. I too wished that I could have done something to make him not do what he did, but I had no control. This, I believe, is the hardest part of dealing with guilt; realizing that I was powerless, realizing that I can't go back and change it. Realizing that the only way for me to go now, is forward via my past.

My guilt swung from being angry with myself to giving God the blame and guilt. It's very hard to separate the sinful action in your mind when you are so close to it. It's easier if you look at it from a 3rd party view. For if someone came to me and said they were being physically abused and were blaming God for that, I would pose the question as it was posed to me. "Who is the one that is actually physically abusing you? Is it a person or is it God Himself." The answer without fault always comes back to it's the person. The next question I too had to ask was, "but then why is God allowing it?" This is one of the biggest dividing factors I have seen in myself and in other abuse victims. Deep down we all wanted God to ride in on a white horse and strike down the person before we ever experienced any suffering. It is a nice thought and that would be a wonderful world to live in, however that is not the reality of the fallen world we live in. God gives each person choice, a choice to do good or bad. Choose to love Him or hate Him. Some people choose darkness over the light and then sin. They enforce their own brokenness onto the world by hurting others. This is not what God wants for us. This is not what He ever wanted for us and thus that is why He sent Jesus to come and pay the price once and for all. When someone hurts you it indeed hurts God. When you hurt someone it hurts God. His heart is full of goodness for us. This is why God restores what has been stolen from us again and again.

"God, your God, will restore everything you lost; he'll have compassion on you; he'll come back and pick up the pieces from all the places where you were scattered." Deuteronomy 30:3

Shame

Shame is like molasses that sticks to you everywhere you go. I can't stand the feeling, taste or presence of shame over me. Neither can anyone else who has this. It has been one of my biggest enemies. Sin and shame go hand in hand with each other.

Whenever there has been sin, shame is present. The spirit of shame is a powerful force that makes one believe they will never be good enough to move forward in life and have blessings. It's like being stuck in a place with no door. However, this is a cheap ploy for the enemy to keep you from God. Have you thought about why it is that all abuse victims suffer with the exact same symptoms? You can travel from the US to Singapore, to the heart of Africa or to the heights or the Himalayan mountains; every single victim of abuse suffers shame and guilt. This is because Satan is a non-creative being and has one cookie-cutter way of trying to destroy people's lives. The only problem with his plan is that he is short sighted and God is not. Have you ever noticed that no two people's story is the same whom God has restored from sexual abuse? That is because God is the creative one and the healer of all, who can deal creatively with each situation. The Devil will try and use lies and mistruths to make you feel unworthy or not good enough, but they are all lies, every single one of them.

I felt a tremendous amount of shame about my story.

It hurts to face myself. I'm ashamed of a lot of things. I have hurt a lot of people. I have hurt me, but this is me, broken, hurt, ready for God.

—Journal entry, 26 June 2008

(*Keeping Secrets*, **Ilonka Deaton**)

God our Father's plan was never for us to experience any of this in the first place. By all accounts it's not something we will ever be able to live with, and be okay with. Your secrets carry tremendous power to have effects on your life. Personally, the effects of my secrets, as I internalized them, were 30 pounds of weight gain first, then depression and anxiety followed. I got physically sick a lot and my gut was in bad shape. After that, my external behavioral choices such as drinking, smoking and drugs took place. It all had a domino effect. There is never one effect when you keep secrets. As I walked into my adult life, I had buried my own self so far down with my secret that I had no idea who I was. This greatly affected my relationship with God. I kept people at arms length. I lied, manipulated and pretended to be someone else. When we hold secrets, it begs for pretention rather than being real. My mind was so focused and made up to keep my secret that I slowly sacrificed myself for it. Was it worth keeping my secret for 12 long years? Absolutely not! The single most effective deceitful method of the enemy is to make you believe that you need to hold secrets that could destroy you and make you sick. He wants to destroy every beautiful thing God has ever created. We can't allow that. Clothing yourself in the truth of who God says you are in His word will help shield you from these attacks and arm you with the truth and wisdom to know when to surrender your deepest hurts to the Lord.

Alcoholics Anonymous has a saying "you are only as sick as your secrets," I think this saying can be applied to all secret keepers' lives. Again, it is only when we surrender those secrets that we find our *secret freedom* in Christ.

The story of Maya Angelou moves me each time I read or think about it. Maya was sexually abused and raped by her mother's boyfriend, a man named Freeman. She told her brother, who told the rest of their family. Freeman was found guilty but was jailed for only one day. Four days after his release he was murdered, probably by Angelou's uncles. Angelou became mute for almost five years, believing, as she stated, "I thought, my voice killed him; I killed that man, because I told his name. And then I thought I would never speak again, because my voice would kill anyone…" (Reference Wikipedia)

Quite often we make silent secret agreements and decisions in our mind that do not reflect the truth about the situation we are in. I think it's always a good idea to question our thoughts and weigh them next to what God says about us. This way our secrets and hurts can be healed by the all-powerful truth we find in God's word.

There is no shame or condemnation if you have kept a secret that has had any kind of physical or emotional effect on your life. I just don't want you to be stuck there. I want you to experience freedom and healing and, most importantly, for you to see how beautiful your story and scars really are.

Prayer

>*Merciful Father, comfort us now. I ask that you will open our hearts and hands to surrender to you the effects that our secrets have had on our bodies and minds. Give us the courage to trust you with the deepest parts of us. Thank you for loving us always. Thank you for healing us. Walk this journey with us step by step and provide your guidance. In Jesus Name, Amen.*

Discussion Notes

In the previous chapter, I asked you to journal about two questions. How are you suffering in secret? What are the origins of your secret?

The next two questions I want for us to address is:

How have your secrets affected you physically and emotionally?

Which part of being affected by your secrets are you struggling with the most?

Answer at your own pace. Give yourself the space to think and feel as you ponder these questions. Each of your thoughts and feelings matter. Take your time. Then, when you are ready, move forward.

I believe in you and I am so very proud of you! You can do this!

Phase II

Facing The Tragedies of Your Past

Chapter 4

Your Story

Claiming and Owning Your Story

"Owning your story is the bravest thing you will ever do"
–Brene Brown

I can vividly remember the first time I shared my story in a small group with about six other women. My church was doing a study called Gospel Transformation. In the study, it invites your small group to allow each participant a one-hour slot to tell your entire story from start to finish. You also could use photos or letters or any kind of object to bring to the group to share. We each had our one-hour slot schedules weeks in advance to give us some prep time. I was so anxious and nervous to tell my story. I though, why would any one care about my life? Little did I know that the group of women would find encouragement by seeing God's hand at work through my brokenness. Gathering pictures and letters brought back so many good and yet uncomfortable memories for me. As I shared with my small group I could feel that each word spoken gave me just a little bit more freedom than the one before. As I was sharing my story I passed photos of my life around the group. I shared with the group that one of my biggest regrets was that I never got to dance on my Dad's feet. In fact, I never got to dance with my Dad. At the end of my one-hour the women spoke life and encouragement into my story. One woman, who has become a dear friend, drew my attention to her.

"Ilonka, you shared that you regretted never having the opportunity to dance with your dad. I want to show you something."

She turned one of my pictures around, a picture that I brought with me. It was of me dancing with my Dad on my 21st Birthday. I had no memory of it. I had completely forgotten. It shocked me to realize that maybe there are faulty things in my thinking that I remember incorrectly. That's when I realized that I needed to study my own story to see with adult eyes what my life was really like. The response and prayers I received were so healing to my heart. Knowing that five other women who had their own stories would take the time to sit for an hour and listen to mine built confidence and brought a newfound hope for me.

This was a necessary step I needed to take to claim and to own my own story. It is difficult to claim and own your story when you have not shared it or when you have not spoken it out load.

Claiming and owning your story will be a key step you will need to take. Maybe you have already done this and you are well on your way. Maybe you have thoughts about it but the task seems too daunting. Claiming your story and owning it is nothing more than you accepting and saying, yes, this is me, this is my story with all it's brokenness and beauty. With that said, I do realize it is no easy task to endure. Sounds easier than what it is… I know. Take heart that if I can do it, you can. Claiming and owning my story took some time. I would say it's a process that I am still in. Each season brings something new to look at and that's ok. We are all in the sanctification process and it's a life long journey with the Lord.

Jesus told us in John 16:33 *"I have told you these things, so that in Me you may have peace. In this world you will have trouble. But take heart! I have overcome the world."* He knew that we would face suffering and troubles and He also knew that only when we find His peace in it we will be okay. The beautiful thing about owning your story is that you make peace with it and accept it. I know we all have things about our past that we would like to change but we can't. Rather we can ask the Lord to help us accept our stories in totality and help us glorify Him through our stories.

Allow me to make some suggestion from my own process in how you too can claim your story.

1. Pictures say a thousand words. Go through your photo albums and gather some pictures from different times in your life.
2. Walk through your home or living space and pick the first object that draws your attention.
3. Gather a couple of items that have great meaning to you. A letter, piece of jewelry, book or memoir, whatever has significant meaning to you.

At this point I want you to pause and work on gathering these three steps. Take your time and when you are ready, let's continue.

Great! You have some photos, an object that drew you and a couple of objects that have significant meaning to you. Now place them all in front of you and let's pray.

Father God, I thank you with so much humility for each story and memory that these objects represent. Please guide us gently through this process and bring your healing step by step. I also ask that you will allow us to see the good and joys in the midst of our stories. May each memory, thought and feeling reveal more of you Jesus. Amen.

Discussion Notes

Looking at the objects and photos in front of you. I want you to pick two at first. Any two. Then decide which one you will start with. Go ahead and get your journal handy.

If you picked a photo I want you to study it. Look to see what was going on at the time and go to your memory of what was happening that day. What story does this photograph have to tell you? What do you feel when you look at it? What time in your life does it represent and how? Write down anything that comes to your mind about this photo.

If you picked the first object that drew you as you walked through your living space, I want you to look at it. Study it. Why do you think you were drawn to it? What story does it tell you and how does that relate to you? What do you feel when you look at it? Write down any thoughts and feelings you experience as you remember.

If you picked an object that has great meaning to you, I want you to write the story of why this object means so much to you.

As you work your way through this process, please know that it does not stop with only two objects. This is just to get you started in processing your life's story. As you feel comfortable you can do the same with all the other objects.

Go at your own speed and when you are ready, move forward.

Chapter 5

Facing Your Past

Facing the tragedies that brought you to where you are

"Jesus went into the tomb, so that we can be raised out of it".

–Tim Keller

Standing at our merchandise table after a speaking event in which I shared part of my story, I saw a woman hovering around in the background. She would come closer and then withdraw again. Eventually I saw she had arranged for a friend to purchase my book for her. She never made it all the way up to my table and when I moved toward her direction she walked away. I knew that she had something to say but it was not the time for her to share. As we left the event that afternoon, she walked right pass my husband and I, gave me a smile and said thanks for the message. She quickly disappeared out of sight but she stayed on my heart the rest of the day. Many months passed and I would wonder about her. One day, I opened up my mail and there was a message from her. I have her permission to share with you what she said. For confidentiality her name and location has been changed. We will call her Bell from California.

"Hi Ilonka, I don't know if you remember me from speaking in California. I wish I had the guts to come up and speak to you. It has taken me many months to read your book. After I read the back page I knew I had to read it, but I was afraid. Your story has so many things in it that happened to me. I have felt so alone and so broken. When you shared your story that day it gave me hope that maybe I too can find the healing you found. I am writing to say thank you for writing your book. Although it has been hard to read it has been good for me. It's still difficult for me to even think about what happened to me but I now see that I too need to step into facing my past so that I can get well for myself. I have decided to start counseling and I have shared with my husband what happed with me. He has been very supportive. I might never see you again but I just

wanted to say Thank You. Your bravery to share has given me the permission to open up".

"This is why I do what I do, so that others can find comfort in Jesus just as I did. Jesus comforts us so that we can comfort others with the same comfort He has given us." 2 Corinthians 1:4.

It took great courage for Bell to read my book and to write me. Facing the tragedies of our past is no easy task, but it absolutely can be done. I love how Tim Keller puts it; "Jesus went into the tomb, so that we can be raised out of it". Meaning Jesus died to give us Life, to give us Hope, to give us Healing. He makes all things new. He uses any broken story and turns it into beauty.

Facing the tragedies of your past starts with you making a conscious decision that you are going to face your story. You do this a little at a time, with the help of counseling, journaling, story writing and support. There is no reason why any of us should be trapped as prisoners to our past when Jesus gained for us freedom from our hurts. Many times I have been asked by women to pray that they can forget their past. I understand this feeling. I have actually prayed that before. The only problem with this is that if we forget our past, we won't see where God was and is in it. When we turn to face the tragedies of our past we will find Jesus in all our stories. That's the beauty and the healing power of it. Your secret freedom is finding Jesus in the midst of your suffering. For each step, heartache, sadness and joy filled moment you will remember, He is in it and with you to heal your heart.

My hope for you is that you, like Bell, will choose to start your journey in facing the tragedies of your past.

When we face our past often a season of grieving comes up. This is normal and to be expected. Grieving is your body processing your pain. In my book *Keeping Secrets,* I talked about the five different stages of grief and what I walked through.

Grief is an essential part of healing. I didn't think I needed to grieve because the violation happened so many years ago, but I was only suppressing it. I needed to grieve so that I could give the 12-year-old girl in me her voice again. When soul wounds are created in us, weeping cleanses out the wound. I like to call them melting tears—melting the old to make way for the new. My grieving process has taken many forms. It has also taken time. For just as the process of grieving is for someone who has lost a loved one, it is the same when you grieve over any loss you have personally experienced. Swiss-born psychiatrist Elisabeth Kubler-Ross, in her book *On Death and Dying,* popularized a five-stage model of grieving based upon her research into how terminally ill persons respond to the news of their terminal illness. Her five stages have since been used worldwide to describe all grief responses. I wept a lot during each of these phases and grew even more. Hope was alive in me. I knew that.

A Researched-Based Model of the Grief Process

1. **Denial:** This is the shock reaction. "It can't be true!" "No, not me!" We refuse to believe what happened. It's hard to face your story. It takes a courage that comes from God. For me, the first step was to be willing to say, "God, I don't know how to go through this, but you do. Please help me."

2. **Anger:** Resentment grows. "Why me?" We direct blame toward God, others, and ourselves. We feel agitated, irritated, moody, and on edge. This is natural. Where a problem can arise here is when you don't communicate with your spouse or loved one as to what you are going through. In my case, Bill knew what was going on with me, and knowing it gave him greater mercy for me during this time. Being angry is ok. God is a big Man and can handle your anger. The key is to give it to Him in this time and to not hold onto it. I love music. Music truly is my life. It is not a cliché. But in those first few months, I left it alone. I chose rather to read the Bible, to take walks with Bill and talk about what I had read, asking question after question, going where my fascination led me. I was young in the Lord, hungry, eager, green, and with a wound as big as the Grand Canyon. I didn't know it at the time, but there is a certain grace afforded to a new believer, like me, a protection that is like a shield around me. I still couldn't look at myself in

the mirror, and I still suffered emotional fallout from all those years, but I felt the peace of God, a steady calm in the midst of the storm that had been my life.

3. **Bargaining:** We try to make a deal with God. God, if You will speed this up I will be a super human for You. Insisting that things be different, like somehow the loss can be undone. This was a hard one for me. For at first I wanted to change my story, but the further I walked into healing the more I became grateful that God could use my story to help others.

4. **Depression:** Now we say, "Yes, me." The courage to admit our loss brings sadness (which can be healthy mourning and grieving) and/or hopelessness (which is unhealthy mourning and grieving). I began to grieve for the 12-year- old girl I had been. We would recover together, she and I. This particular stage looked a bit different for me. When God took my depression away the day He saved me, it never came back. My depression phase of grieving looked more like admitting that this was my story. I was sad, but I did not fall into despair and depression. It's not that depression is bad or something to be ashamed of. This phase was just different for me.

5. **Acceptance:** Now we face our loss calmly. It is a time of silent reflection and regrouping. "Life has to go on. How? What do I do now?" My gaze turned once again to 2 Corinthians 1:4, "He comforts us in all

our troubles, so that we can comfort those in any trouble with the comfort we ourselves receive from God." My story is meant to help others. That is what makes my story okay. That is how I accepted my past and how I have been called to move on, for each one of us is a missionary in this world, here to help someone else.

These five stages are just to give you a guideline and to show you that you are not alone in your process. What you think and feel is okay. God reminds us that there is a season for everything under the sun.

> *"To every thing there is a season, and a time to every purpose under the heaven:*
> *A time to be born, and a time to die; a time to plant, and a time to pluck up that which is planted;*
> *A time to kill, and a time to heal; a time to break down, and a time to build up;*
> *A time to weep, and a time to laugh; a time to mourn, and a time to dance;*
> *A time to cast away stones, and a time to gather stones together; a time to embrace, and a time to refrain from embracing;*
> *A time to get, and a time to lose; a time to keep, and a time to cast away;*

A time to rend, and a time to sew; a time to keep silence, and
a time to speak;
A time to love, and a time to hate; a time of war, and a time
of peace."

–Ecclesiastes 3: 1-8

Heavenly Father, our pasts hold so many memories that
can be hard for us to remember. Holy Spirit please guide
each thought and memory and bring Your healing Jesus
into those difficult places. Open our eyes to see where you
were and are in our stories and give us the courage to
face our pasts. Comfort us now and walk with us.
In Jesus' name, Amen.

Discussion Notes

In the previous chapter you wrote about objects and pictures
that brought memories back to you. For this section I would
like for you to journal your thoughts and feelings about the
following two questions:

What do you feel when you think about facing the
tragedies of your past?

What would your tomorrow look like if you were able to
face some of the things in your past?

Take your time and sit with the Lord. Quiet your mind
before you write and invite the Holy Spirit to guide you. You
are and never will be alone in this process. God promises that

He is with you. You can do this! When you are ready, move forward.

Chapter 6

Naming Your Need

Listening to your heart's desire and acting upon it

"I have a great need for Christ; I have a great Christ for my need."

–Charles Spurgeon

S eptember of 2007 was one of the darkest seasons in my life. It was the month that I attempted to take life into my own hands and tried to commit suicide. For months leading up to that day the evidence of my depression was clear as could be. I could feel it but I would not admit it. I held on tightly to the denial that I can fix myself and that I didn't need help. My arrogance almost cost me my life. Being stuck in such a dark place, it's easy to take on the mentality of always being a victim. That was me. I was a victim in life. I felt the world was out to hurt me and that I was the only one that could steer my ship. I was self-centered, arrogant, obnoxious and even self-righteous. Back then I would have never dared to pick up a phone to call a self-help line to save my life. I didn't think I needed that kind of help. I thought that kind of help was for the *really* troubled person. Yet I *was* the really troubled person. There were many things that led up to my attempted suicide, but the day that broke the camels back was especially a dark day. The record company that I was signed to at the time let all their artists go. Bill moved to California. My Mom wanted to disown me after reading a letter that Bill wrote to her in my defense. It was just a crappy day and way too much. I ended up in a psychiatric hospital for almost two weeks and I thank the Lord that I did not die that day and that I finally got a hold of my denial. *The complete account of this day is documented in full detail in my book "Keeping Secrets."*

Denial is a powerful enemy that will make you believe things that will harm you. It is so important that we listen to our heart's desires and name then. If you can't name your need, it can't be helped or healed. I had to get to a place of naming what my needs were. I had to confess my utter brokenness and pain so that I could get better. I understand what it's like to think I can handle whatever life throws my way, but that's not the truth. I can't. I need Jesus with every breath I take. God exposed my need for Him through this terrible situation. I pray that you do not have to go through what I did to express your need. It's okay to need help. It's okay not to have all the answers. It's okay to say, "I am broken." It's okay for us as believers to need as much as we did the day He saved us. It is through our openness to this brokenness that we heal.

Do not be afraid that you will fall apart if you let go to allow God to help you. Jesus told us 365 times in the Bible to not be afraid. *"Do not fear, for I have redeemed you; I have summoned you by name; you are mine". Isaiah 43:1.* The fear of the unknown healing that can take place in your life can be scary. I use to be afraid of it as well. After walking through my process for the past 11 years I can tell you with honesty that it's not easy, but it certainly is easier than the hell I was living in before. It's like walking down the road that has both sides of it on fire. The fire can't touch you. It can't burn you. You have no way around it but only to keep on walking toward water and the light of day in front of you. You sweat and you get uncomfortable. With every step you are a little closer to the daylight. With every step you gain a little more courage. With ever step you heal and you become free. When you get to the daylight and you look back you think, "It wasn't as bad as I thought it was going to be". Then you realize that the healing and freedom you gained by placing your entire need on Jesus was so worth it.

Expressing our needs and listening to the desires of our hearts gives us the opportunity to act upon it.

Precious Jesus, thank you that you died for us. Thank you that you constantly pursue our hearts. Thank you that you care this much about us. Lord, you know how hard it is for us to sometimes let go of our need and to trust you with our hearts. Please help us now to trust you and allow you to heal the broken parts. Give us the courage to name our needs and give us the ability to be still so that we can hear the desires of our hearts. In your matchless name we pray. Amen.

Discussion Notes

In the previous chapter we addressed facing the tragedies of your past. For this section I would like for you to journal your thoughts and feelings about the following two questions:

What needs do you have?

What are the desires of your heart?

If you find yourself struggling with this section, pause and pray. Ask The Holy Spirit to help you. It's okay to take your time. When you are ready, move forward. I am praying for you even now as the Lord will lead you.

Resources for counseling and help line needs are listed in the back of the book.

Phase III

Finding Comfort

Chapter 7

Repentance

Crying for help and turning to God to find comfort

The Apologist's Evening Prayer

–C.S. Lewis

From all my lame defeats and oh! Much more
From all the victories that I seemed to score
From cleverness shot forth on Thy behalf
At which, while angels weep, the audience laugh;
From all my proofs of Thy divinity,
Thou, who wouldst give no sign, deliver me.
Thoughts are but coins. Let me not trust, instead
of Thee, their thin-worn image of Thy head.

From all my thoughts, even from my thoughts of Thee,
O thou fair Silence, fall, and set me free.
Lord of the narrow gate and needle's eye,
Take from me all my trumpery lest I die.

O h the turning of a repentive heart bares both difficult and delightful moments. You have heard people talk about reaching the end of themselves or hitting bottom when they refer to a turning point in their lives. The word repentance has a different meaning to different folks. If you grew up in a hell fire and damnation church, you'd probably think of repentance as something you have to do so that God wouldn't strike you down. If you grew up like me in a Dutch Reformed Church, who held tightly onto the legalistic way of approaching God's word but yet are elected, you might feel that it's hard to do anything right and repentance becomes such a word that carries shame. At least that is how I experienced my church back then. Or, maybe you grew up having a gentle understanding of God's grace and the word repentance meant meeting Jesus with open arms. Either way, we all have a different view of what repentance should and would look like. I too, like many others before and after me came to that point. I will never forget the day I repented. One of our retiring pastors at Christ Community Church where Bill and I have been going to since 2008 told me this in a conversation one day.

"There are a million ways to Jesus, Ilonka, but only one way to the Father"

–Pastor Scott Roley

His statement opened my mind to realize that we all have a different story of what repentance looked like for us. Our experiences with Jesus are all unique. I am so fascinated to hear how someone came to know the Lord and how that moment, whether it was as a child or an adult, gave way to an eternal relationship with Jesus. When I think about the word repentance, I think of turning and changing directions. This is what my experience was like. I still feel like it was yesterday when I turned to Jesus.

Spring of 2008 Bill and I had just left the 2nd Sunday Service at Christ Community Church in Franklin. On our way home we made conversation, going over details of the sermons as we drove. Our conversation about Jesus then turned into an argument. I can't remember what we were even arguing about. I was so upset. I couldn't control the stirring that started in me since the first time we went to that church. I so badly wanted to cry and let the emotions out of my soul, but I couldn't. I didn't know how. So I took the only course that worked to release my emotions, and that was to argue to the point of no return, and then I could cry. The argument was horrible. A third world war broke out in our house. Hurtful words flew through the air, and we both said things we wished we hadn't. It was awful. It got so bad that I took one of Bill's walking sticks. It's a salvation walking stick that he made in high school shop. It has the colors of the salvation story in marbles embedded in the handle of the stick. Beautifully carved and symbolizing Bill's own salvation when he was a teenager, it was a remembrance of when he gave his heart to the Lord. Embarrassed as I am even now telling you this, I took that stick went downstairs to the garage and tried my best to break the windows of his sports car with it.

Bill tried to calm me down, but he too was upset. He asked me to come back upstairs. The situation was crazy. I was the crazy girl holding his salvation stick. I responded by destroying his handmade walking stick, leaving it in pieces. I didn't know it at the time because I grabbed it out of rage, but it was one of his favorites. Now it was broken, and I had broken it. As it shattered into pieces, I too shattered, and broke one final time to my core.

Breaking Bill's stick wasn't enough. I still had the dress on that I had worn to church, so with both hands I started at my neck and ripped it till it fell onto the floor. In my undergarments and out of my mind, I ran back upstairs and bolted out the front door. I ran toward the street. I was going to throw myself into ongoing traffic and end it all. There was nowhere left to turn. I felt abandoned, broken, and used. My whole past story was coming up to the point of vomit.

Halfway across the lawn, Bill grabbed me from behind. He put a towel around me and held me with a very firm grip.

I couldn't move. He kept me from running into the street. He covered me and carried me back into the house. The neighbors were staring at us at that point. I had made a total spectacle of myself.

Once we got into the house, Bill tried to stand me up, but I was limp and collapsed into a lump on the floor beneath him. I had no power, no will, no energy to stand, completely broken— just like that salvation stick. He knelt beside me, placed his hand on the back of my neck, and began to pray.

"Lord, I don't know what else to do for her."

It was a desperate prayer. He threw his whole self into it. Bill got up to close the front door and to make sure the neighbors weren't peaking through the doors and windows. But when he walked away from me something unexpected happened. Lying on the floor half naked as I cried uncontrollably, I heard a voice. It wasn't Bill's voice, and we had no guests in the house. It wasn't my imagination either. The voice called my name and asked a simple question.

"Ilonka, if he can pray like that, why can't you?"

In an instant I saw a picture of Bill in my mind on his knees praying to God. I didn't struggle for interpretation. Understanding was immediate. I knew by the mere authority and peace that it was God directly speaking to me. Then with all my heart I cried out. It was from the deepest part of me. It was my moment of repenting and realizing that I could not and would not ever be able to save myself from the hell I was living in.

"Jesus, if you are who my mother and my grandmother taught me you are, if you are the Jesus I learned about in Sunday School, if you are who Bill says you are, if you are who these Pastors say you are, you need to come into this house right now and help me because I want to die. Don't send an angel because that would freak me out. You Jesus... you... come and help me."

The words hardly left my mouth when a peace settled on me that I am not sure I had ever felt before. I felt covered, but there was no actual cover over me. It was supernatural. Bill wasn't sure what was happening but helped me to the couch. He then went and got an actual blanket to cover my body. I still have the blanket he had covered me with. I fell into a deep sleep. I slept for 18 hours that night and my life was changed when I woke up. (I think the Lord must have said, "Let her sleep, angels, there's a lot of re-wiring to do here"!) Jesus saved me right there, half naked on the floor in my house. He met me with no condemnation, no shame and no guilt. With open arms He met me with Grace, love and help. The turning of my heart into repentance wasn't as frightening as I always thought it would be. It actually was quite comforting because it took all the pressure off of my shoulders and put it on Jesus, who in the first place bore all of my sins so that my yoke would be light when I am in Him. My depression was gone and has never returned. I saw trees and heard birds sing for the first time since the day I was raped. My personality was different. It was obvious that something happened to me.

This was my moment of repentance and turning to the only one Jesus who could rescue me. From that point forth I have lived a full life of learning and being molded by the Lord daily to be more like Him. It has not always been easy but every step has been worth it because I have victory and hope.

We all have a different experience when it comes to repentance and all of it matters. It is beautiful because it's part of your story.

After a speaking event in Seattle Washington in 2015 a woman came up to me and shared that she felt her story was inadequate because nothing really bad had ever happened to her in her life and she gave her heart to Jesus when she was four years old. She added that she felt only traumatic stories are celebrated. My heart broke for her in that moment. Here she was, a bright lighthouse for Jesus, but due to what society has dictated a "true redemptive story" must be. She thought only a testimony was valid if it was one filled with all the junk someone like me went through. That is such a lie from the devil. I got quiet and gave her the space to talk. When she was done I said. "Lou Ann, the reason someone like me shares my *broken* story is so that others and our children might have *your* story. Your story is to be celebrated on the highest level because that is what we want for our loved ones and children. You are celebrated and you give me hope that together we can make a difference. You are a walking example that bad things, such as what happened to me, do not *have* to happen for a true testimony. I love and respect your story and I am so humbled that you shared your heart with me." I then went on to pray with her and we visited some more.

Your story matters in its entirety! All of it. Your moment of surrender. Your moment of repentance. No matter what it looks like, it matters! Do not allow the fallen world to dictate whether your experiences have value or not. Place your trust in God's word that says *all* of you matters.

> *Precious Lord, I come against the attacks of the enemy on your people. Lord I ask for your protection over our minds and hearts and physical lives. Lord, surround us with your truth and help us to see You in everything. Give us the words to express our painful past and give us the needed portion of faith to turn with repentive hearts to you. In Jesus comforting name I pray, Amen.*

Discussion Notes

In the previous chapter we addressed naming your needs and listening to your heart's desires. For this section I would like for you to journal your thoughts and feelings about the following question:

What has repentance looked like in your life?

Feel free to journal your entire experience. Take your time and when you are ready, we will move on.

Chapter 8

Surrender and Renouncing

Making the decision to come clean with your secrets
and to renounce that secret of your past.

*"Come to Me, all who are weary and heavy-laden, and
I will give you rest. Take My yoke upon you and learn
from Me, for I am gentle and humble in heart, and
YOU WILL FIND REST FOR YOUR SOULS. For
My yoke is easy and My burden is light."*
–Mathew 11:28-30

I surrender all. I surrender all. All to thee my blessed
Savior, I surrender all. These all too familiar words in
the Hymnals of our churches took author J.W. Van
Der Venter five long years to write. Van Der Venter has the

call of ministry in the area of Evangelism on his life. His friends and family could all see it, but he was reluctant to surrender to God. Judson Van de Venter (1855-1939) was raised on a farm near Dundee, Michigan. After graduating from Hillsdale College, he taught art in public schools in Sharon, Pennsylvania. Van De Venter was active as a layman in his Methodist Episcopal Church, including participation in revivals held at the church. Based on his amazing faith and service to the church, friends encouraged him to leave his field of teaching and become an evangelist. It took five years for him to finally "surrender all" and follow the advice of his friends. His ministry took him to various places in the United States, England, and Scotland.

Perhaps the most important influence that Van de Venter had was on the young evangelist Billy Graham. The Rev. Graham cites this hymn as an influence in his early ministry. His account appears in Crusade Hymn Stories, edited by Graham's chief musician, Cliff Barrows. The Biography of J.W. Van Der Venter United Methodist Church.

In his own words Judson described his writing of the song as a struggle. *"The song was written while I was conducting a meeting at East Palestine, Ohio, and in the home of George Sebring (founder of Sebring Camp Meeting Bible Conference . . .). For some time, I had struggled between developing my talents in the field of art and going into full-time evangelistic work. At last the pivotal hour of my life came, and I surrendered all. A new day was ushered into my life. I became an evangelist and discovered down deep in my soul a talent hitherto unknown to me. God had hidden a song in my heart, and touching a tender chord, He caused me to sing.*

There is nothing easy about surrender in any part of your life. Instinctively we all want to self-preserve and be independent. When the knowing is on your heart that there is something in your life that needs to be surrendered to God, it usually results in a nagging thought or feeling that appears again and again on your heart. Surrendering the deepest parts of your heart is not easy. I see it as the equivalent of taking your heart out, placing it in your own hand and saying, "here you go". None of us naturally want to do that. Rather we want to protect that broken place and hide the hurt that happened so long ago. We push down those emotions one more time hoping they might go away. This is all normal. We all want to be protected, covered and loved. The only problem with holding on to what needs to be surrendered is that you won't experience the freedom, the healing and the relief God has for you if you don't surrender it.

When I imagine surrender as a picture in my mind. I see the Lord with open arms inviting me to give Him my burden. I also see his patience in waiting for me when I'm ready. Surrendering your secrets to God is a tender matter. It takes a big step and time. There is no rush or limit on how much time and effort you can spend on it. I know it is uncomfortable too, as I have walked through my own journey of healing and washing of my secrets. I have had to learn that surrendering the parts of my heart wasn't a once and done kind of a deal. Rather it was and is a daily walking with the Lord to invite Him into my broken places. No one can tell you how you should do this or what it must look like. Surrendering your secrets to the Lord will look like none other. The best example that comes to mind for me was when the prodigal son decided to surrender in his circumstances and go home. In Luke 15:11-32 we get to read the loving forgiving story of the Prodigal Son. Many parts of this story resonate with my own heart and story. One area in particular that stood out to me was when the son decided to go home. He tried to make it on his own and came up short. Exhausted, dirty and hungry he finally makes the decision to surrender and to go home to his father. I love that the bible included his thoughts for us as he made the decision to go home.

> 17-20 *"That brought him to his senses. He said, 'All those farmhands working for my father sit down to three meals a day, and here I am starving to death. I'm going back to my father. I'll say to him, Father, I've sinned against God, I've sinned before you; I don't deserve to be called your son. Take me on as a hired hand.' He got right up and went home to his father.*

He had it figured out in his brain. He thought he knew how this was going to play out. Doesn't this sound familiar when we have to surrender we already have an image of what it's going to be like? Convinced of his plan he rushed home. Now here is the beautiful part. Our plans and expectation of what God is going to be like when we do surrender and turn to Him will always be met with a great plan. God will always outshine anything that we can possibly imagine and make it greater. Our own thinking is flawed. Only when we do surrender and experience God's amazing grace do we get to see what He indeed has for us. The prodigal son experienced the same thing. Thinking he was going home to be a hired hand for his Dad, he was humbly and pleasantly surprised that his father had way more for him.

20-21 *"When he was still a long way off, his father saw him. His heart pounding, he ran out, embraced him, and kissed him. The son started his speech: 'Father, I've sinned against God, I've sinned before you; I don't deserve to be called your son ever again.'*

22-24 *"But the father wasn't listening. He was calling to the servants, 'Quick. Bring a clean set of clothes and dress him. Put the family ring on his finger and sandals on his feet. Then get a grain-fed heifer and roast it. We're going to feast! We're going to have a wonderful time! My son is here—given up for dead and now alive! Given up for lost and now found!' And they began to have a wonderful time.*

Our gracious heavenly Father has so much more in store for you. There is no shame or condemnation for the secrets you have held in your heart. None. There is only grace and mercy. Each one of us decides when and where the day is going to be when we surrender those hurtful parts. It's part of your story. My prayer for you is that you will start the journey to move towards surrendering those parts of your heart to the Father. It's not easy, I know. It takes time. It takes effort. It also takes a decision on your part.

> *Heavenly Father, thank you for your help in teaching us how to surrender to you. Lord I ask that you with your gentle hands guide us through this step. Give us the wisdom to know where to start and how to move forward. In Jesus name, Amen.*

Discussion Notes

In the previous chapter we addressed what repentance has looked liked in your life. For this section I would like for you to journal your thoughts and feeling about the following two questions.

Which parts of your story do you still need to surrender?

Use this opportunity to tell the Lord anything that has been heavy on your heart. He will meet you with gentleness and kindness. His Mercy and Grace are plentiful for you. Take your time and when you are ready, we will move on.

Chapter 9

Forgiveness

Birthing new life into your story

"Get rid of all bitterness, rage and anger, brawling and slander, along with every form of malice. Be kind and compassionate to one another, forgiving each other, just as in Christ God forgave you."

–Ephesians 4:31-32

Forgiveness. What a word and task. When I gave my heart to Jesus in 2008, forgiveness was something I truly struggled with. I knew God's Word called me to forgive, but my brain couldn't make sense of it. I thought for the longest time that forgiveness was all up to me. I would read quotes on forgiveness such as, "holding a grudge doesn't make you strong; it makes you bitter. Forgiving doesn't make you weak; it sets you free". I would read quotes like that and think it sounds nice, but how do I do that? How do I muster up the energy and power that is needed to forgive someone? What if I do forgive that person? Does that mean I condone what happened and enter back into a relationship? These are all complicated questions with answers to each, but for a young Christian mind it can be overwhelming. In my frustration and misunderstanding of what true forgiveness is I eventually came up with the only thing I knew I could do. I needed to go to the Lord with it. I had many people and things to forgive in my life including asking for forgiveness for the things I did wrong. However, where I had to start was the strongest point of un-forgiveness against the man who sexually trapped me and abused me for so many years, my ex-music manager.

Some time had passed since that spring day when I cried out to Jesus and my heart was changing. The looming, daunting task of forgiving was hovering over my head like a neon sign reminding me that at every glance in the mirror it was time. I liked running back then. Two to three miles a day made me feel energetic and vibrant. Slipping on my Adidas running shoes, I convinced myself that this run would clear my mind. I just needed to go and run and let all this looming forgiving stuff go. Sounds simple doesn't it, or like I am in denial. As if a run could fix what was hurting in my heart. I set off in the direction of the city running at a nice pace.

With every step I took, my thoughts went back and forth from "It's going to be okay" to "It's time". The ambivalence between my flesh and spirit made me feel like a ball stuck in a pinball machine trying to find home. I kept on running and struggling in my mind. I liked the silence and the road noise of running. No music or interference, just me and my thoughts. This time though, my thoughts were running harder than my legs were working. I became exhausted. Tired of the struggle, I didn't want to have this conversation with myself one more time. I want out, out of this confusion in my head. I reached a traffic light and had to stop due to traffic. I couldn't take one more step like this.

"I give up Lord. I give up. I have no idea how to make this stop or how to forgive John for what he did, but please make this stop. Take this from me and help me. I choose right here and now to forgive him. Please help me to do this."

Little did I know that in my frustration I did the only right thing I could do, and that was to ask God to *give* me the forgiveness that I would need to forgive.

I continued my run and went home. As the weeks and months rolled on I would find myself thinking and being bothered with forgiving. I could tell that I had not forgiven yet. When it would come up I repeated my prayer to the Lord as I did that day at the traffic light.

"Lord help me"

The more I prayed it, the easier it became and then one day I woke up and knew in my heart and spirit that I had forgiven. Make no mistake, *I* didn't do it. *God* did it. All I did was ask Him to help me when I made the decision to want to forgive.

Forgiveness is a process that the Lord walks us through. He knows how fragile and tender our hearts are. He knows how hard it is for us to do the things He wants us to do. That is why the Lord always meets us with open arms to help, and never with a whip. Although we might not see it in the natural realm, God's Holy Spirit physically holds us and walks with us through these difficult parts. I can tell you that for me, I didn't have the power or the strength to do what was needed for me to have the kind of forgiveness for my perpetrator. Only God could have done that.

I love the poem "Anyway" by Mother Teresa. I think of it often when I find myself in need of the Lord's help, because forgiveness is always between you and God.

Mother Teresa's Anyway Poem

People are often unreasonable, illogical and self-centered;
Forgive them anyway.
If you are kind, people may accuse you of selfish, ulterior
motives;
Be kind anyway.
If you are successful, you will win some false friends and some
true enemies;
Succeed anyway.
If you are honest and frank, people may cheat you;

Be honest and frank anyway.
What you spend years building, someone could destroy
overnight;
Build anyway.
If you find serenity and happiness, they may be jealous;
Be happy anyway.
The good you do today, people will often forget tomorrow;
Do good anyway.
Give the world the best you have, and it may never be
enough;
Give the world the best you've got anyway.
You see, in the final analysis, it is between you and your God;
It was never between you and them anyway.

Please hear me when I say I know how hard this is. None of the things we are talking about in this book is easy. You are not alone and never will you be. The Lord gives us directives in the Holy Word to help us. It's always us living under God's grace getting a helping hand from Him. He finished the work so that we can rest and ask for his help in carrying our heavy loads. The scripture in Ephesians I referenced earlier is amazing and I like to read it with a personal twist to make it my own. Let's try this together as a prayer.

Gracious loving Heavenly Father, please help me today to *get rid of all bitterness, rage and anger.* Please give me the ability to let go of all *brawling and slander, along with every form of malice.* Guide me to *be kind and compassionate to others.* Help me to *forgive each one; just as in Christ God forgave me.* Thank you for your kindness and love and for being here when I need you. In Jesus precious name I pray, Amen. *Ephesians 4:31-32*

Discussion Notes

In the previous chapter we addressed surrendering to the Lord. For this section I would like for you to journal your thoughts and feelings about the following two questions.

Who hurt you that you still need to give forgiveness?

What part of your story do you still need to find forgiveness for yourself?

Write it all and be bold. If you are stuck and unable to name what is in your heart, pause and ask The Holy Spirit to guide you. Come back and pick your journal when you are ready and try to write again. Give yourself grace to move at your own pace. The Lord is with you in all of this. I am even now praying for your heart to meet the heart of Jesus in this forgiving process. I believe in you and I know you are going to experience a great freedom through this. Take your time and when you are ready, we will move on.

Phase IV

Now What?

Chapter 10

The Importance of Writing Your Secrets and the Story that It was Held in

Putting your story down on paper

"Now at last they were beginning Chapter One of the Great Story which no one on earth has read: which goes on for ever: in which every chapter is better than the one before."

—C.S. Lewis

Your story matters! Every word of it! Using your own voice to express the path you have been on will not only help in your healing process but also remind you of how important your story is. Dr. Dan Allender reminds us in his book "To Be Told" that every story of this earth needs to be told. I have often spoken on the importance of how our life stories reveal to glory of God to other people. One of my favorite Bible stories that illustrate this perfectly is the Woman at The Well talking to our precious Jesus. After she and Jesus had been speaking for a while, the Samaritan women left and went back to her village calling attention to this wonderful man she had just met.

"Come see a man who knew all about the things I did, who knows me inside and out." John 4:30

Then this is the part of the story that gets me every time. See here how Jesus used her broken story to draw many to Himself in that community. Jesus was glorified through her story.

Many of the Samaritans from that village committed themselves to Him because of the woman's witness: "He knew all about the things I did. He knows me inside and out!" They asked Him to stay on, so Jesus stayed two days. A lot more people entrusted their lives to Him when they heard what He had to say. They said to the woman, "We're no longer taking this on your say-so. We've heard it for ourselves and know it for sure. He's the Savior of the world!" John 39-42

The Lord loves to use what we think are the worst parts of our stories to draw people to Him. Never sell yourself short or underestimate the power of your story. Sharing what God has done in your life will bear the life of Jesus to others. You are a light-bearer and hope-holder for others.

Learning how and what to share takes time and effort on your part as your journal your secrets and the story it was held in. You see our secrets are important, but the story surrounding your secrets is what gives it the space to express your pain and to find your voice again in the midst of your own story.

Throughout this book I have asked you in every chapter to journal. The reason I do this is because journaling sends a signal to your brain while you are writing that "this is important." You are in fact giving wings to your story and allowing your voice to be heard.

Journaling also gives you a private space to express. As we unpack the secrets of our past and our stories, there are many healthy boundaries to be learned along the way. Not everything should be shared. The first rule is to keep yourself safe in the process of unpacking your story. Give yourself the privacy that is needed to honor yourself. This is a good thing. It means that you care about the journey that is your life and place value on it. There is an incredible book on boundaries that you can read to find practical solutions on how to have healthy boundaries. *"Boundaries. When To Say Yes and When To Say No." by Dr. Henry Cloud and John Townsend.* I recommend this read if you do not understand boundaries or are still struggling with it. I still reference my own copy when I find myself in a situation that needs clarity.

So how do you write the story of your life? You write it a little at a time. Just as you have been writing your thoughts and feelings, you start slow and easy and you write what is on your heart that day, whatever that may be.

I offer a couple of suggestions that could help you decide how you would like to write. There are many different types of thinkers and writers, here are three that I have come across when speaking at conferences.

Analytical Writer. If you find that you are someone who likes to make a list and stick to your 1 through tens, then an actual writing list might be helpful to you. Write down the bullet points or big life markers that comes to mind and work down your list one at a time. This way you will feel that you know where to go and you won't be so overwhelmed with years of information in your head.

Creative Writer. If you are someone that is like me, a creative thinker that doesn't necessarily need structure to start but are rather led to write by feelings, then I recommend you write what you feel the day you sit down to write. I'll give you a piece of advice that my dear friend and author Patsy Clairmont gave me when I wrote my first book. Use file folders and mark them each time you write to signify the timeline in your life. I would for instance sit down to write and have the relationship with my mom on my heart. I would write till I felt I was done then take those pages and put them in a folder labeled "Mom." This method helped me in my own creative thinking pattern write down all I needed to say without getting overwhelmed and yet still maintain some sort of a system.

'I Don't Write' Writer. Many people are more audible and don't like to write. If this is you, that is okay. As much as I would like to urge you to step out of the uncomfortable and try writing, I also don't want you to get stuck and not process your story. A small tape recorder or computer program might just be the tool for you. There are many dictation software systems that you can use to speak your story or you can simply record it on a voice recorder and still use a filing system to keep track of your own story line. Whichever works for you, it's okay. I actually spoke and recorded my entire story onto a program called Garage Band before I ever sat down to start writing it bit by bit using the folder system.

Whichever method works for you, go with it. The important part here is that you engage and journal in some form. Your story is too beautiful and your voice needs to be heard.

Father God, thank you for our beautiful broken stories. Please help each one of us to unpack and write what is needed for that day. Give us the courage to say what is needed and weep through the pain. Comfort us with

your love as you heal our hearts. Thank you for the
freedom that is ours through Jesus. Amen.

Discussion Notes

In the previous chapter we addressed forgiveness. For this section I would like for you to journal your thoughts and feelings about the following two questions.

Where would you like to start with your story?

What system of writing do you think you will use and why?

I am excited with you in this journey you are on. Take your time and when you are ready, we will move on.

Chapter 11

Unwrapping Your Shame, Guilt and Condemnation
Finding Freedom in God's Truth

"Therefore, there is now no condemnation for those who are in Christ Jesus."

–Romans 8:1

There is absolutely no shame that we need to carry when we are in Christ. Satan wants you to feel shame. He wants us to think that we need to carry the weight of our sin, for where there is sin there is shame. He knows that if he can somehow convince us that it's ours to carry, the weight of our sin would cause tremendous shame. I am here to tell you today this is a lie and an absolute ploy that is not from our Lord.

Jesus didn't just partially die for your sins. He died for all of it and that includes shame, guilt and condemnation. When God the Father looks at you, He sees Jesus. Because of his magnificent grace we get to live a life free from shame, guilt and condemnation. When God looks at you precious one, He does not see a failure. He sees a victorious child.

About a year ago I was doing a publicity tour for my book by visiting television stations, doing interviews on what the Lord has done in my life and pointing others toward the hope of Jesus. We had just come back from doing a TV Segment on the Steve Harvey show about an anti-human trafficking film that my husband and I worked on. Steve Harvey was very nice by the way, and so funny! I was able to share Jesus on national television and so did Steve! It was a wonderful experience.

The last stop of our publicity tour was with a well known Christian television station. We arrived at the station early that morning for hair and makeup. I was pretty pregnant at that point and wanted to take some extra time to pull myself together for the interview. It has never been easy for me to share my story. Although this is what God has called me to do, it has not become any easier for me to share the darkness of what can happen in this world. In sharing, I look forward to the moment when I can talk about Jesus. It's like a fresh boost of energy when I get to that point. I am reminded each time I share of how amazing the Hope of Christ is in my life.

The interview went great that morning and the staff was pleased. I made my way to the dressing room to change into some travel clothes, as we would be traveling home right after. On my way toward the dressing room a Pastor who was also there that day came up to me.

"Ms. Deaton. I was wondering if I could just have a moment of your time."

"Sure."

"Thank you for sharing your story today. It resonated with my heart. My sister who is currently 37 years old was trafficked in her early twenties and has since gotten stuck in a forced life of prostitution and drugs. We have tried several times to get her out of the situation, but her traffickers would show up at our family's home and threaten to kill us. My mom and I are very worried about her and we do not currently have a location on her. My sister is too afraid to share any information like that. I do however have a secret video account that she will occasionally call me on. I was wondering if you would find it in your heart to please record a video message to her on my iPad that I might be able to get to her at some point. I think if she could hear your story then maybe she too can have the courage to get out."

My heart broke into a million pieces as this pastor was sharing his sister's story. I could feel the hopelessness and the darkness. I could see an anticipated hope in his eyes.

Without hesitation and with a deep knowing in my heart I knew I wanted to do this.

"Yes. Absolutely. Give me your iPad and I'll record it right now."

I walked off to the side to find a quit spot and poured out my heart to this women. Pointing her to the hope of Jesus and encouraging her that she too matters so much. When I finished I prayed and asked the Lord to somehow get this to her and to give her the courage to step out in faith and get out of this situation. I handed the pastor his iPad. My husband Bill exchanged phone numbers with him and we traveled home. On our way home it hit me. Oh my goodness…what if her pimps see my face or my name. I surely am always an advocate of being safe and protecting myself. I didn't even think about it. My gracious loving hubby turned to me with gentleness and put his arm around me.

"The Lord will protect you baby. You did the right thing here and they would have to come through me. It will be okay."

He then went on to pray for me and it reminded me that Satan doesn't want me to help anyone. He wants me to be afraid and the fear I was feeling was coming from him, not the Lord. I rebuked his cowardly effort and thanked God for the opportunity.

We arrived home safely and relieved for a well-spent trip of ministry. We weren't even home a couple of hours when Bill got a call from that pastor at the television station.

"Mr. Deaton, my sister is willing to give me the location and she wants out. I sent her the video of Ilonka and she cried the whole night. So much so that her pimp beat her up for having a cried-out looking face. My sister told me that if Ilonka could do it so could she, and that she was ready for help."

"Praise God pastor! I am so thrilled to hear this! Let me go ahead and share some information with you about a couple of different organizations that we work with who do rescue operations."

Bill shared contact information with the pastor and made some introductions. This all happened swiftly. When you find yourself in a situation where someone is willing to get out of that life or willing to share a location, time is of the essence. Well, to make a long story short, less than 24 hours later, the Pastor's sister was rescued and placed in a safe house. All the pimps that were on site were arrested as well as two dirty cops. All have since been charged with human trafficking and drug charges. Remarkable. I am still so astounded that God allowed us to be part of this woman's story. She is still in recovery and doing well. Her road is hard but she is committed. Finding the hope of Jesus was everything to her.

You see, Satan wanted her to feel ashamed of her life. Guilty for what she was part of. Condemned by society because of her actions. She never chose this life. She was trafficked and that became all she knew. When the human spirit is broken, the only way to put it back together is with

Jesus. That's exactly what has happened for her. None of us can take any of the glory for her rescue or redemption. Only Jesus can. But we can thank Him that He so graciously allows us to be a part of others' stories to help them.

Don't allow the enemy to make you believe that you are guilty, that you have to feel ashamed or that you stand condemned. I know this pattern of thinking can take a while to change in your mind. God's word will wash your mind to renew the way you think. I too thought that I had to carry the shame, guilt and condemnation. It took daily devotions and audibly repeating what God really says about me to have my mind renewed. My thoughts were so far off base that I actually had to write out a script that I kept ready. I kept doing it to such a degree that I wrote a song called "Wash" with my dear friend Gary Forsythe about this very topic.

WASH

I say that I'm in chains
You say I'm free

I say that I am stained
You say I'm clean

I say that I'm ashamed
foolish and weak

You say that I'm forgiven
You died for me

Let your words wash over me
Let your words wash over me
Let your words wash over me
Help me believe

You say I'm not alone
That you'll never leave

You say I'm beautiful
You sing over me

You're say that you're enough
To make me complete

Father, you're faithful
to hold on to me

You say that I am free
You say that I am forgiven
You say that I am clean
I'm beautiful

Ilonka Deaton. Lonki Lou Publishing. Gary Forsythe. Collision-Point Publishing. Copyright 2013.

In addition to writing this song I also used the following script. It's not an original concept that I came up with, but one I adjusted to fit my situation. There have been many sermons and teachings that have used similar ones to this. If you struggle with shame, guilt or condemnation please feel free to use this or create your own as you are led.

What God Says vs. What I think

You say: 'It's impossible'
God says: All things are possible
(Luke 18:27)

You say: 'I'm too tired'
God says: I will give you rest
(Matthew 11:28-30)

You say: 'Nobody really loves me'
God says: I love you
(John 3:1 6 & John 3:34)

You say: 'I can't go on'
God says: My grace is sufficient
(II Corinthians 12:9 & Psalm 91:15)

You say: 'I can't figure things out'
God says: I will direct your steps
(Proverbs 3:5-6)

You say: 'I can't do it'
God says: You can do all things
(Philippians 4:13)

You say: 'I'm not able'
God says: I am able
(II Corinthians 9:8)

You say: 'It's not worth it'
God says: It will be worth it
(Roman 8:28)

You say: 'I can't forgive myself'
God says: I forgive you
(I John 1:9 & Romans 8:1)

You say: 'I can't manage'
God says: I will supply all your needs
(Philippians 4:19)

You say: 'I'm afraid'
God says: I have not given you a spirit of fear
(II Timothy 1:7)

You say: 'I'm always worried and frustrated'
God says: Cast all your cares on Me
(I Peter 5:7)

You say: 'I'm not smart enough'
God says: I give you wisdom
(I Corinthians 1:30)

You say: 'I feel all alone'
God says: I will never leave you or forsake you
(Hebrews 13:5)

Father, thank you that you have given us the truth of Your Word to stand on. Thank you that we can be reminded of just how much You truly care and love us. Nothing in this world can ever compare to the love, mercy and grace you have for us. Please help us in our unbelief to believe the things that you say about us. Help restore our hearts and minds to be more in line with your truth and help us change the lies that we have believed from the enemy into the truth of who You say we are. Your marvelous word is life to our souls. Thank you Lord. In Jesus name, Amen.

Discussion Notes

In the previous chapter we addressed writing your secrets and story. For this section, I would like for you to journal your thoughts and feelings about the following two questions.

In which way do you struggle to believe what God says about you?

What area in your life do you feel has an element of guilt, shame or condemnation that still needs to be dealt with?

Dig deep into this one and take your time. When you are ready, lets move on. I am so proud of you for doing this! Stay in there! You are not alone and you can do this!

Chapter 12

Seeing Your True Identity

Reclaiming your voice and learning
how to fly again with a wounded past

*"You belong to God, my dear children. You have
already won a victory over those people, because the
Spirit who lives in you is greater than the spirit who
lives in the world".*

–1 John 4:4

W ho are you? This is one of the deepest questions
you will ever face. Wrapping our hearts around
the fact that God actually does have a plan for
our lives (Jeremiah 29:11) is a truth we need to hold onto.
After spending time with many other women at church and

in bible studies, I quickly came to realize that I was not alone in my heart's cry to find out who I am. Many of you today have asked this question or felt this way and it can be a very lonely place to get stuck. Once we admit that we too are feeling this way, we can start the conversation of what God is telling us and what the purpose is of our heart's cry. We all have a place where we belong. This is a question that God so graciously answers for us. *Isaiah 43:1* says *"Fear not, for I have redeemed you; I have summoned you by name; you are mine"*. Your identity is rooted in Christ. For many of us, our pasts can sometimes be such a heavy burden that we think it defines us, but it does not. There is nothing in this world that can ever dictate who you are, for the truth of your identity, value and worth was already established before you were born by Christ. You have identity because Christ has identity and you are in Him.

You mean so much to God. He calls you His. (Isaiah 43:1) This is pretty spectacular. This means that you have a freedom available to you from any discouragement this world can bring. Who you are rests in who God created you to be. You are a beloved daughter of God bought by the blood of Jesus so that you can live your life to the fullest. *John 10:10* says *"I have come that they may have life, and have it to the full"*. Jesus came so that you can have an abundant life. The desires of your heart, the personality you have or what you find beautiful are uniquely yours. God doesn't make mistakes and He surely created one special person in you. To compare yourselves to others is so destructive to your souls. We are eagerly encouraged in Proverbs 4:23 to guard our hearts… *"Above all else, guard your heart, for it is the wellspring of life"*. You *must* guard your heart. It is not ok for any of us to continually break our spirits down by comparing ourselves to others. Have you ever noticed when you are standing in the grocery checkout line, and you are staring straight into all the glamour magazines, you never seem to feel better about yourself? You end up judging your weight, your hair, or whether your children are dressed like celebrity children; if your teeth are white enough or if you have the latest clothes on. Somehow within seconds it turns into a self-doubting party of "I'm not enough". This is what the Lord is talking about by not being conformed to this world. *"Do not be conformed to this world, but be transformed by the renewing of your mind, that you may prove what is good and acceptable and the perfect will of God… Abhor what is evil. Cling to what is good"*. Romans 12:2

All of this comes back to who you are. Who God says you are. If you know the truth about who God says you are in your heart, it's easier to arm yourself against untruth and discouragement. But what if you don't know you are? What can you do and where do you go with that? You seek to find out who you are.

Setting out to find who you are can be a very fearful step to take. I know. I too had to go through this process. Not knowing who you are is frightening. Don't be afraid! Who you are, and what God created you to be, is always for the good and so much better than what we can imagine. The words "fear not" is roughly mentioned more than 314 times in the Bible. In Mark 5:35-36 we read about the synagogue ruler whose daughter had died. Jesus' words to him was "Don't be afraid, just believe." Today these words are true for you because Jesus loves you. Don't be afraid if you don't know who you are, God will show you. If you want to know who you are you must ask to know and for God to show you. "Ask and it will be given to you; seek and you will find; knock and the door will be opened to you". Matthew 7:7. This is a giant step of faith to take, but if you are willing to trust the Lord, He will show you the beauty of who you truly are. Seeing yourself in the light that God sees you will be comforting and transforming to your soul. This is an exciting journey, not one that harms you. We all get injured in life but the good new is that Christ redeems that for us. His grace is always sufficient.

Did you know that an injured bird normally does not bleed readily (the way mammals do)? This happens because they cannot afford to loose much blood. Avian blood clots very quickly when exposed to air, unless a vein, artery, toenail, or blood quill has been damaged. Their feathers actually hide a multitude of sins. Generally in order to see a bird's wound, each feather has to be moved aside to expose the skin underneath. Furthermore, birds are masters at hiding their injuries and are programmed to act normally when in distress, this is to protect themselves from predators.

For most of us, we have found an injured animal at some point in our lives. Taking care of an injured bird is very similar to the process God takes with us when we have been wounded and need attention. Just like the bird we are all sometimes far too good at hiding our wounds and our feathers have to be pulled back one at a time to see our bruised wounds.

God cares very much about the wounds of your past. The wounds that I pray will become scars of beauty in your life. The process of taking care of those wounds, just like with an injured bird, is to first create a safe and warm environment in which you can start to be fed and healed. There is no healing outside of God's protective hands. When we try to do self-healing it never works.

Take for instance the Samaritan woman at the well. Her story no doubt has devastation and trauma in it as she has been married so many times. Seems like she had been trying to find her place in this world by going from relationship to relationship. When she met Jesus, He broke all the rules to speak with her. Not only did He start telling her the truth, knowing full well her story and sins, but also instead of asking her for water, He offered her "living water". With love and compassion Jesus ministered to her heart and had one of the longest conversations recorded. The fresh miracle of her Jesus encounter sent her running back to her community where she breathlessly announced, "Come and see a man who told me everything I ever did." Scripture records that not only did men from that community come to see this man Jesus she was talking about, but also Jesus ended up spending two additional days ministering to this community. When He was done many people became believers. They said to the woman, "We no longer believe just because of what you said; now we have heard for ourselves, and we know that this man really is the Savior of the world."

You see, her past opened a door for her to reveal the glory of God to other people. It is through our wounds and our scars that we get to comfort other people. Not only will God comfort you and heal your hurts, but He will also use those same wounds to encourage and comfort others. Our wounded past is not only something we have to get over or finally get through, it is the very key to how God will use us in others' lives. For it's the mother who has had an abortion who can comfort another with the same pain she has experienced. It's the woman who understands the atrocities of being violated sexually who can comfort another who has a similar story. We all try to understand each other but nothing speaks so clearly of God's comfort as our own wounded, broken past filled with stories of pain and redemption. No matter what your story holds, or what you have been through, there is a redemptive purpose in it.

If you heart is still in a place of deep hurt I urge you to start the recovery process. Finding the safety of Jesus in a community of people that will not judge you but walk with you is essential. This might look like you starting to write your story out or to engage in conversations with a counselor.

Whatever your process, I know that God only has the best for you and your healing is part of it. Once you are stronger and your wounds have become scars, you too will become a warrior for other wounded hearts. God comforts us with the same comfort we get to provide to others.

It is okay to go through this process or exploring your voice and identity with God. When we do this we choose Life. We choose to be more. We choose to press deeper into God. We choose to allow ourselves to grow. This is a beautiful process that will allow you to bloom. Our identities, our values, and our worth have always already been established. It is just hard sometimes to see it when life gets distorted and we loose our way. The good news is there is always a way back into the knowing of who we truly are in Christ and how to reclaim our voices again to fly with the freedom we have been given.

> *Jesus, we need your help to understand daily what it means to have our identity rooted in you. Please give us the wisdom to understand and the eyes to see. Give our minds the ability to accept that which You say of us and transform our hearts and minds to be more like you. Give us the courage to use our voices and the ability to fly again in the abundance of your love. In your precious name we lay ourselves at your feet Jesus, Amen.*

Discussion Notes

In the previous chapter we addressed guilt, shame and condemnation. For this section I would like for you to journal your thoughts and feelings about the following two questions.

Who are you?

What are your shattered dreams that have prevented you from singing a new song and flying again?

Be kind to yourself in this process. Don't be so hard on the mistakes you have seen in your life. Mercy and grace is not only for the other person, but also for you. We tend to let self-contempt set in and harden our hearts to the very life we ought to be living. Allow yourself to rest in the peace that Jesus has for you as you find your new song. Take your time and when you are ready, let's move on.

Chapter 13

Using Your Secrets, Your Story and Your Voice to Comfort Others

Going forward to make a difference

"Don't be ashamed of your story, it will inspire others."
–Anonymous

I often get asked if I love sharing my story publically. The question brings up many different responses in my heart and mind. Speaking about what I went through isn't easy and it came with a big learning curve for me. What I do love about it though, is sharing what Jesus did in my life. It lights a firecracker in my belly when I get to talk about Jesus. To get to that point though, I have to show the darkness that disappeared when light walked into my life. So yes, I guess

I would say I love to share my story, especially the hopeful parts. The darkness that once was in my life is a reminder each time of how much I still need Jesus everyday. As I have shared over the years, what has made my story worth it is that fact that it helps others. It took me while to realize that we all are walking examples of 2 Corinthians 1:4. God comforted me so that I can comfort others. For that reason, I do what I do. *"He who comforts us in all our troubles, so that we can comfort those in any trouble with the comfort we ourselves receive from God." 2 Corinthians 1:4*

I love how The Message Bible describes it as *The Rescue*, *"All praise to the God and Father of our Master, Jesus the Messiah! Father of all mercy! God of all healing counsel! He comes alongside us when we go through hard times, and before you know it, He brings us alongside someone else who is going through hard times so that we can be there for that person just as God was there for us. We have plenty of hard times that come from following the Messiah, but no more so than the good times of his healing comfort—we get a full measure of that, too." 2 Corinthians 1:3-5*

God comforts us so that we can comfort others. Part of His comfort for others lies within the suffering of our stories. The glory lies in the redemption of that same story. The light that points to the cross is the hope that we get to carry to others. Therefore we must share boldly what is true to be ours, our own story. Not each person is called to a public life of sharing. I know in my heart that I am, and I will walk out that calling leaning on God's mercy as I continue. For most, sharing your stories is for the community and family around you. You never know how the Lord will use your story to help someone else. God turns our sorrows into beauty and shows others He will do the same for them. How glorious is that.

I want for you to get to a place where you can use your voice with confidence to share your story. I want for you to be able to spread your wings and fly as high as you can. I want you to succeed! I want to see you do well in your life. I want to see you sing a new song from your heart that is called freedom. Everything that you have gone through matters! Everything!

Now you might think that it's easier said that done, but please know that with God all things are possible in your life. You have what it takes already. As you have stepped into this process you have already started spreading your wings to fly and lifting your voice to sing a new song of freedom and redemption. I know the work isn't easy, but it's so worth it.

So how do we fly again…with a new song as you walk through this?

"He has given me a new song to sing, a hymn of praise to our God. Many will see what He has done and be amazed. They will put their trust in the LORD."
Psalm 40:3

Did you know that birds are not born knowing how to sing? They learn their first songs from their Fathers. In most bird species males are predominantly the ones to sing. Although females do have the ability and do sing during certain seasons, it's primarily the males you hear from your window in the morning. I used to think that birds sing because they are so happy and that they are light-hearted creatures. However, their singing is much more complex. I have a bird app on my phone that allows me to record and recall which birds are in our trees at any given time. Watching and listening to birds is one of my favorite pastimes. Our home sits on about two acres of land surrounded by trees and attracts all kinds of singing birds. One particular birdie that I love is the Northern Mockingbird.

The Northern Mockingbird is also known as the Mimus Polyglottos, which means "many-tongued mimic" from the Latin language. It's name refers to the many different songs and calls this bird can imitate. It has over 200 songs it can sing. It also often gets bored and imitates others birds or makes up new songs. Although each species of bird has their own song, no two neighbor's song sounds the same as they change it slightly to mark territory. The mockingbird is also a really good parent. They mate for life and the males help the females build a home nest, feed their young and help nurture them. Learning about that remarkable bird reminds me of our Heavenly Father and how He sings over us.

In the book of Zephaniah we get such a clear picture of God our Father singing over us as He quiets us with his love. Can you imagine God's voice? I often do. It must be remarkable. Think about the best singers in the world and all the magnificent birds that can sing, all of which only have an extension of God's singing gift. Wow. I am mesmerized at the idea that I will one day, with you, get to hear how lovely God's voice is. His voice is more than only a song or a sound; it has the power to transform your mind and heart. It brings hope, just as it did in the time of Zephaniah who lived in a very disheartened world filled with idol worship, child sacrifices and darkness. Zephaniah came and brought a word of light and life about God's good news. This same encouragement and hope is extending to you who are in Jesus Christ. God sings over you with joy and loves you.

The world around you has a lot of darkness in it. It can be very disheartening to stand in the midst of a broken world. The truth still holds fast that God remains in control, singing over you and calling you out to dream and sing with Him. You too can be the light in a dark place. God has given each one of us a calling and a dream. Too often due to the fray of life we forget to continue dreaming, to create a new song and to expand our creative life with God himself. God is one of love and life and wants just the best for us. All of your broken dreams and forgotten songs can be revived into a new redemptive song.

You might have lost your voice somewhere in the middle of life's struggles. I know what this feels like. It can be very scary to step out and find your voice again so that you can sing a new song. The good news is that you do not have to do this alone. God will help you. All the dreams and desires of your heart are just as important to God as they are to you. You are never alone nor ever forsaken in this world. Every part of you matters! You are that precious to God!

I needed a new song in my life. As I was finding my own voice again, while going through trauma therapy about my abusive past, I learned that it is a process. The first step I had to take was being willing to name the hurts of my past that took my song away. As I started naming them one by one, I invited Jesus to help me walk through them. I did not take all of them at once, but one at a time like a baby birdie learning to fly again. It took great patience and a constant daily prayer of asking God to help me press deeper into a new redemptive song. I did not try and control the speed I was going but honestly put it in God's hands to lead me. There is something so beautiful when we lean on Him to lead us.

Look at Bathsheba. She's the mother of Solomon who has the story of all scandal. Boy did she ever need a new song. Her story gives us so much hope that no matter what the circumstances have been in your life, God can and will redeem it. No matter what you have done or what has been done to you there is forgiveness in Jesus with bundles of grace. Our only position should be to surrender all of this at the feet of

Jesus for healing. That way we can all learn a new song to sing, use our voices boldly and lift our wings to fly.

I had the great opportunity to write a song with my husband and my dear friend and mentor Patsy Clairmont, who wrote a poem that inspired me to put my voice to it. This song/poem is for you.

Fly Again
LOVED…
Still

Oh look at you turned to stone
Perched near the window sill
You look away as if to say
Your shame has made you still

I want to help you fly again
To lift your voice to sing
But I for one know
A heart can break
And it's not easy to take flight

Fly again
On the wings that He gave you
Will carry you up safely
And on and on and on
You must fly again

Above the storm that rages
Beyond the tear stained pages
Up to the Holy places
Cause your Savior loves you still
You must fly again
Yeah…

The winters come and gone
The clouds give way to life
Without the weight of regrets raw cry
It's so easy to take flight

So fly again
On the wings that He gave you
Will carry you up safely
And on and on and on
You must fly again
Above the storm that rages
Beyond the tear stained pages
Up to the Holy places
High above the storm
You gone fly again yeah

One day you'll take
The flight of your life
You'll lift up your wings and sing
You're gonna fly again

Lift your voice

Spread your wings

High above the sky

Beyond the tears

Your Savior still loves you

Hold on tight

Hold on to Him

Your Savior loves you

Still

© 2015 Written by: Patsy Clairmont, Ilonka Deaton (Lonki Lou Publishing BMI), Bill Deaton (Queen Takes Pawn Publishing BMI)

Father God, thank you for the life you have given us through Jesus. Help us to dream again with you. Put a new song in our hearts. Comfort the very broken pieces that have kept us from singing again and heal us so that we are able to worship you through our new song. May this song be the light for many others around us. Amen.

Discussion Notes

In the previous chapter we addressed shattered dreams. For this section I would like for you to journal your thoughts and feelings about the following two questions.

How would you like to fly again in your life?

What song would you like to sing as you use your voice again?

Be bold in your approach and request in this task. Dream and write all that is on your heart. When you are ready, let's move on. I am so proud of you!

Conclusion
A Word to You

"Courage is not the absence of fear, but rather the assessment that something else is more important than fear."

–Franklin D. Roosevelt

My heart can be reminded a thousand times a day to not be afraid and still I will need to keep God's word close to my heart to not fear. You have started such an amazing task. To say I am only proud of you would be an understatement. I am so humbled by your bravery to step into the healing the Lord has for you. I know this is no easy task and yet here you are doing it! Each step you have taken is so worth it. The freedom you are finding will be yours forever. The forgiveness you experience will bring you great peace and the Father's love that surrounds you will continue to comfort you.

At this point, I can say for you to go ahead and give yourself a tap on the shoulder and say, "I'm doing it!" Yes you are! In a big way! Each of us has the choice to continue stepping forward and you are doing it.

Don't give up on this journey because the words in this book are coming to a conclusion. Press forward with your story. Keep stepping onwards and exploring all that God has for you. Wrestle if you need to wrestle in the harder things. Grieve where you need to grieve. Laugh till you cry. You matter! You have always mattered.

Keep on choosing Life! Jesus came so that we can have life and have it more abundantly to all it's fullest *John 10:10.* Instead of staying numb to your broken dreams and unfulfilled aspirations, step out into Life and Live again! Rest in His presence and allow yourself to find a new voice with a new song. Jesus already did it all for us! Our only part is to believe on the things that He has done for us.

Graciously explore the parts of your heart that still need forgiveness. God calls us to forgive and He gives us the ability to do so. You are not on your own when it comes to this very difficult task. Forgiveness and forgiving is mentioned roughly 150 times in the Bible. This is a big deal because it affects us greatly. When we walk in unforgiveness, it brings anger and bitterness that can take root in your heart and keeps you grounded, not being able to fly. I want you to fly again and soar with a new song. For if Jesus were standing in front of you, you would hear the words, "you are forgiven completely". The beauty of forgiveness is that it will always remain that the Father God helps you to do this. We can't forgive ourselves because we do not possess the gift of it apart from God giving it to us. But rest assured that He gives it *freely* to you. Step forward with Him and continue to have your heart healed from those who have harmed you and for the mistakes that you might have made.

Continue to be kind to yourself. Don't be so hard on the mistakes you have made in your life. Mercy and grace is not only for the other person but also for you. We tend to let self-contempt set in and harden our hearts to the very life we ought to be living. Allow yourself to rest in the peace that Jesus has for you as you find your new song. Gentleness and patience yields great fruit in this healing process. It is not about the big changes that you see, but about all the little ones that add up.

When you find yourself feeling stuck, take a break and come back again. This is a marathon, not a sprint. Pacing yourself according to what your body needs is wise. Not every hurt and story in your life will have a neatly tied bow around it. Not every story and hurt will have resolution, and that is ok. The point is to get you to a place of having peace about your story. I still have unresolved parts of my story that I now have peace about. In 2012 my husband and I went back to South Africa to file charges on the man who held me in slavery for so many years. It was a difficult process to walk through, but I did it. Since then the case is still open and I do not know what the outcome will be, but in my heart I have peace. I know I did what I needed to do regardless of the outcome. The forgiveness I have gained is priceless even if I don't have earthly resolution yet. We don't always get to see the final results to each thing we have gone through and that's ok. The point is not to wrap everything up, but for God's redemption of those parts to be bigger in our life.

I will continue to pray for you as you journey forward. Don't give up! If you find yourself needing further help, please use the references in the back of this book.

My prayer for you as you keep on stepping forward is that Jesus will make himself known to you on a deeper level everyday. That your body, mind and spirit will be healed, set free and redeemed from anything that still holds you captive. May you experience the Father's love in a bold new fresh gently way. May your dreams, desires and aspirations come to fruition. May you wake up everyday knowing that you are so deeply loved. May the Lord bless you and keep you. May He shine His face upon you and be gracious to you. May He forever give you His peace. *Numbers 6:24-26.*

In Jesus name, Amen.

Facilitator Notes for Small Group Leaders

Tips for Leading a 'How to Fly Again' Small Group

Thank you for your willingness in accepting the challenge of leading others along their own journey as they learn how to fly again.

PREPARATION

Be prepared. Being well prepared will give you the confidence you need and alleviate any anxiety you might feel about leading the group. Have the goals of what you would like to see happen in the group well thought out and planned. Your preparedness will not only help you lead well but will set everyone else at ease.

Be a good facilitator. A good facilitator is simply being a good role model. Be on time. Do your homework. Be uplifting and positive. Maintain strict confidentiality. Be a good listener. Be consistent with how long each week's session will go and stick to it.

Know your limitations. You are not personally responsible for the outcome of each participant. All you do as a good facilitator is to point people to Jesus. You can't "fix" anyone. You are a helping guide to walk along side your participants. Each individual in the group is responsible for their own growth.

Pace the group. Be patient in your leading but stay on schedule. Should you find one participant taking over all the conversation of the group, do not be afraid to take control back and lead others in the discussion. You might say "I would like to talk with you after the group to continue what you would like to share". This way you respect everyone's time but also validate the participant who might need to share more in depth.

GROUP SIZE

I recommend no more than 5-7 people in each small group. If you have a larger group, go over each chapter together and then break into small groups. Each small group should have a leader to facilitate the questions. For a group of no more than 5-7 people you will go over the chapter and questions in the same group without breaking into a smaller group. Once participants have signed up and you have done an introduction week, the group should be closed to any further participants wanting to join. Make sure to give your participants a signup deadline. This will ensure that confidentiality will remain within the group once you have started.

GUIDE RULES

It's important to set your guide rules at the very first introduction week. You can write these guide rules down and give them as a hand out. Here are some examples you can use:

Welcome to our small group. We are so glad you are here to join us. To make this a meaningful and productive small group, here are some guide rules we will follow each week.

- Our small group is confidential. What we share as a group stays within the group.
- Group members are not required to talk but are encouraged to do so.
- Agree to accept and to encourage each other.
- Be on time.
- Be respectful of each other's time.
- Do not give "fix it" advice. We are all in it together.

LENGH OF TIME FOR THE SMALL GROUP

- You may decide how long the group will meet. I do not recommend shorter than an hour or longer than one and a half hours.
- You can decide if you would like to meet for one chapter each week, which would be 13 weeks. Or you can do two chapters each week with an introduction week.
- You can decide to have some refreshments each week or have a sign up sheet for participants to bring

something each week in rotation. Should you have refreshments, encourage participants to arrive 10 minutes early.

- *from the group leader*: Should you have any questions or need to talk through the course of this group, please feel free to reach out to me. Thank you, and I look forward to walking through this journey with you.

FACILITATING EACH WEEK

In your first meeting you will not cover any material. Introduce everyone to each other and go over your guide rules. It's important to lay out the structure for the next several weeks as well as the expectation of each participant. Use this time to get to know each other. Encourage participants to share a bit about themselves.

LEADING THE SESSION EACH WEEK

- Start with some refreshments if you have chosen to do that.
- Open with prayer.
- Go over the guide rules.
- Open a general discussion by reading the chapter title or titles that are being covered that week and ask for thoughts and feelings about it.
- Guide the conversation then do the questions for each week.

- Allow 5-10 minutes at the end for any prayer request.
- Close in prayer.

CLOSING THE GROUP EACH WEEK

It is very important to stay on time each week. Manage your time wisely. Strive for consistency by starting each session on time and ending on time each week.

WRAPING UP YOUR SMALL GROUP STUDY

Coming to the end of a small group study such as this can be pretty emotional. I recommend planning your last week after the study is done as a celebration week of encouragement. I like to call it the "We did it" celebration. This will bring closure and a sense of accomplishment to your participants. A good visit after so much hard growth work has been done will be delightful to each participant's heart.

Acknowledgements

Writing a book takes a village. I would not have been able to endure this process if it were not for key people who helped me along the way.

Thank you Father God for your grace and mercy. You Lord, alone, have allowed me to share my story with others. I am eternally grateful to you for my salvation in Jesus Christ and this new free life I am able to live.

My Wonderful Husband, Bill

My love, no one has allowed me to walk out the suffering of my past and explore my story more than you. Your countless hours of listening and support have allowed me to become the woman I am today. Your diligent prayers and passion for what Jesus is doing in our lives portray the kindness of the Father himself to me. I admire, appreciate and love you. A simply thank you can never be enough for how you have weathered this storm with me. Thank you for your encouragement to press forward and write a second book. Thank you for being an amazing father to our precious children. You have showed me Jesus and walked out his grace in front of my eyes. You are one of a kind and baby you are my one.

My Messy Family

We are a glorious ridiculous awesome messy family. Mom, thank you for being the "you can do it" voice in my head. Thank you for loving your grandchildren and for helping me when I need you. To my bothers Jaco, Bjorn, heavenly family Dad and grandparents, and extended family, I am so glad God chose me to be part of this family. We indeed have a wonderful redeemed story. We all can tell of God's love in our lives and the work He has done in us. I love each one of you and hold you dear in my heart. I have such fond memories of each of you. Thank you for your support, love and willingness to be open to the healing Jesus has done in our lives.

My Publishing Family and Friends

Karen Anderson, thank you for believing in me. I love your boldness! To David Hancock and the entire Morgan James Publishing House, thank you for being part of my journey and for giving my words flight. To all my close friends, supporters and readers, I appreciate your prayers and I adore your love. You help me in this journey of life and show me Jesus. Thank you!

References

Introduction
Psalms 51:4 (NIV)
2 Corinthians 4:2 (NSV)
Psalms 34:18 (NSV)
2 Corinthians 1:4

Chapter One
Quote by Cassandra Clare
"Keeping Secrets" Ilonka Deaton 2016

Chapter Two
Quote Anonymous
Psalms 121:1-2 (NIV)
Romans 8:1 (NSV)

Chapter Three

Quote C.S. Lewis

"The Wounded Heart" Dr. Dan Allender 2008

Genesis 3:6-11 (NIV)

Deuteronomy 30:3 (NSV)

"Keeping Secrets" Ilonka Deaton 2016

Wikipedia: Maya Angelou

Chapter Five

Quote by Tim Keller

2 Corinthians 1:4

"On Death and Dying" Elizabeth Kubler-Ross A Researched
 Model of the Five Stages Of Grief

Ecclesiastes 3:1-8 (NSV)

Chapter Six

Quote by Charles Spurgeon

Isaiah 43:11

Chapter Seven

"The Apologist Evening Prayer" by C.S. Lewis

Quote by Rev. Scott Roley

Chapter Eight

Matthew 11:28-30 (Student Bible)

Wikipedia "The Biography of JW. Van Der Venter of "I
 Surrender All"

Luke 15:11-32 (Student Bible)

Chapter Nine
Ephesians 4:31-32 (NSV)
Mother Teresa's *Anyway Poem*

Chapter Ten
Quote by Cs. Lewis
"To Be Told" by Dr. Dan Allender
John 4:30 (NIV)
John 39:42 (NIV)
"Boundaries" *When To Say Yes and When To Say No*, by Dr.
    Henry Cloud and John Townsend

Chapter Eleven
Romans 8:1 (Student Bible)
"Wash" by Ilonka Deaton Lonki Lou Publishing (BMI) and
    Gary Forsythe Collision Point Publishing (ASCAP)
    Copyright 2013

Chapter Twelve
1 John (Student Bible)
Jeremiah 29:11 (Student Bible)
Isaiah 43:1 (NIV)
John 10:10 (NSV)
Proverbs 4:23 (NIV)
Romans 12:2 (Student Bible)
Matthew 7:7 (NIV)
Psalm 40:3 (NSV)

"Fly Again Devotional. How To Fly With A Wounded Past"
by Ilonka Deaton & Patsy Clairmont

Chapter Thirteen
Quote Anonymous
2 Corinthians 1:3-5 (The Message Bible)
Psalm 40:3 (NSV)
"Fly Again Devotional. How To Fly Again With A New
Song" by Ilonka Deaton & Patsy Clairmont
"Fly Again...Loved Still" by Ilonka Deaton Lonki Lou
Publishing (BMI) Bill Deaton Queen Takes Pawn
Publishing (BMI) and Patsy Clairmont

Resources

Ilonka Ministries P.O. Box 681334 Franklin, TN 37068
  www.ilonkaministries.com

Focus on the Family (Local Christian Counseling) www.
  focusonthefamily.com 855-771-4357 (US) 1-800-681-
  9806 (Canada)

To find a local counselor in your area visit www.211.org

Centerstone (Suicide Crisis Call Center) 1-800-273-8255;
  24/7/365

Child Abuse Access: www.childhelp.org 1-800-4-A-CHILD
  (24-7)

Cyber Tip Line Report child exploitation http://www.
  missingkids.com/cybertip

Celebrate Recovery (10 Week Support Program) Issues: Any
  addictions, hurts, or habits (age 18 and older) Find a
  support group by state- www. celebraterecovery.com

Door of Hope 4 Teens Issues: Self Harm (cutting) Access:
  www.doorofhope4teens.org

Texting 4 hope: 914-393-1904 615-746-7319 Email:
doorofhope4teens@gmail.com

Finding Balance (Advice on Eating, Body Image, and Life)
Issues: Eating Disorders and Cutting/Self-Injury
www.findingbalance.com

IAMACHILDOFDIVORCE
Issues: All issues for families going through divorce
http://iamachildofdivorce.com/L.I.F.E.MinistriesIntern
ational

Freedom Everyday
Issues: Sexual Addiction Access: www.freedomeveryday.
org 1-866-408-5433 (Ext. 5)

National Runaway Switchboard 1-800-RUNAWAY (1-800-
786-2929)

National Trafficking Hotline 1-888-3737-888 National Safe
Place- text "SAFE" and current location to 69866 to
receive the name and address of the closest Safe Place;
www.nationalsafeplace.org.

National Domestic Violence Hotline Issues: Abuse,
Domestic Violence Access: 1-800-799-SAFE (7233)
www.thehotline.org

National Child Abuse Hotline. If you need help or have
questions about child abuse, call the Child help
National Child Abuse Hotline at 1-800-4-A-CHILD
(1-800-422-4453) then push "1" to speak with a
counselor.

Option Line (24/7 Pregnancy Centers Nationwide) Issues:
Pregnancy, abortion, rape, relationship (sexual), STDs
(male and female) Access: 1-800-712-HELP (4357)
www.optionline.org

Out of Darkness: 24/7 RESCUE Issues: Pornography
industry, Stripping, Survival sex, Prostitution, Sex
trafficking Access: www.outofdarkness.org Phone Access:
24/7 RESCUE Hotline: 404-941-6024

RAINN (Support for Victims of Sexual Assault)
Issues: Sexual assault/abuse, child abuse/sexual abuse,
rape (partner, acquaintance, stranger), dating and
domestic abuse, hate crimes, incest, sexual exploitation
by helping professionals, sexual harassment, stalking
www.rainn.org Phone Access: 1-800-656-HOPE (4673)
/ Available 24/7

XXX Church (Pornography and Sexual Addiction Support)
Issues: Pornography, sexual addiction Access: www.
xxxchurch.com FREE Accountability Software: http://
www.x3watch.com/x3watchfreebuy.html

Books

"The Wounded Heart" by Dan B. Allender, PhD.

"To Be Told" by Dan B. Allender, PhD.

"Boundaries" by Henry Cloud and John Townsend

"Unveiled Hope" by Scotty Smith and Michael Card

About the Author

Ilonka Deaton's inspiring message of hope is one of victorious life for any individual who has a wounded heart trapped in secrets. Growing up in South Africa, she was held in sexual slavery bondage for five years through the threat of her and her family's life. Now set free and redeemed, she sings and speaks to audiences across the U.S. She encourages individuals through the love of Jesus Christ and reminds them that their stories matter.

As an author, Ilonka has written *"Keeping Secrets" One Women's Story from Sexual Slavery to Freedom*, as well as co-authored *"How to Fly Again Devotional" with author Patsy Clairmont from Women of Faith.*

As a recording artist, Ilonka has eleven recorded albums, performing internationally, and also collaborating and performing on projects with artists including Michael W. Smith, Jill Philips, Rebecca St. James, and others. She has a degree in Biblical Counseling. In 2012, she and her husband opened a free counseling center in Nashville for hurting women. She is a loving wife and mother of two beautiful children. She also loves her Yorkie, scrap booking, a warm sunny day, and fly-fishing with her husband. This is her second book.

Morgan James
Speakers Group

www.TheMorganJamesSpeakersGroup.com

We connect Morgan James published
authors with live and online events
and audiences who will benefit
from their expertise.